APPLEBY
ON ARARAT

APPLEBY ON ARARAT

By

MICHAEL INNES
(John Innes Mackintosh Stewart)

GREENWOOD PRESS, PUBLISHERS
WESTPORT, CONNECTICUT

1

Miss Curricle set down her book and peered through the plate-glass of the sun-deck café.

"The sky," she said, "is cloudless and intensely blue."

The tone might have been thought needlessly instructive, for the atmospheric fact was obvious and—near the tropics—unsurprising. Or there might be sensed behind Miss Curricle's didactic habit some administrative tradition in the family; just so in the nineties might her father, closing a file at five o'clock, have announced yet another meritorious enactment enforced.

"*Intensely* blue," reiterated Miss Curricle, again with a satisfaction suggesting that an invisible brush of her own had collaborated in this loaded effect. "Mr. Hoppo, you have observed the sky?"

Mr. Hoppo sat up with courteous alacrity; the movement constricted some invisible garment at his neck; his forefinger, hesitating, betrayed the absent clerical collar; as the unnecessity of the question struck him his features took on an overplus of benevolence.

"Yes, indeed. It is quite remarkable." He stretched in his seat, so as to bring into view—what is not always easy on a great liner—a strip of sea. "And the ocean too"—

he spoke as one who will inevitably broaden the intellectual basis of any discussion—"the ocean too is quite remarkably blue—quite extraordinarily so. Possibly only the Bay of Naples—"

"The ocean," said Miss Curricle briskly, "is not so blue as the sky." Miss Curricle, perhaps because only glass and white paint and sky were visible to her and she had no intention of stirring, disapproved of the introduction of a rival element. "The *sky* is *intensely* blue. The sea too is blue—but less so."

"I find I cannot agree with you. From where you sit I suspect your view to be imperfect. If you were to move this way—"

"Thank you, but it is scarcely necessary. The ocean makes no momentary change of its aspect in this part of the world." Miss Curricle wriggled her behind more firmly into her chair, meantime preserving a hazardous minimum of ladylike poise in her unflinchingly squared shoulders. "And I observed before sitting down that it is less blue than the sky."

"Less luminous, perhaps. But in point of sheer intensity of colour . . . ah, a whale!"

From her seat near the soda-fountain Mrs. Kittery giggled nervously—evidence of a power of swift perception behind her large and unspeculative eyes.

Miss Curricle turned back from the rail to which she had hurried.

"I cannot see a whale. Nor, Mr. Hoppo, do I believe

that there *was*, in fact—"

Mrs. Kittery removed from her mouth the straw through which she was sucking lemonade.

"Everything is blue," she said largely and eagerly. "The sea and the sky and what they dress the boys in. It's peaceful, I suppose. But sometimes I feel it gives you the blues, all that blue. I feel it would be nicer really—*more* restful —if the sea was green. Like a great big field."

"The sea," said Miss Curricle, seizing the opening, "*is* green. Most distinctly so. A *pure* blue is characteristic only of the firmament. Salt water is colourless in itself, or is possessed of a slightly greenish tinge. On shipboard, this may be observed in the bath."

Mrs. Kittery's straw bubbled dangerously. Miss Curricle, with a glance at Mr. Hoppo which seemed to admonish him to await further instruction where he sat, turned towards this new adversary.

"Mrs. Kittery, are you quite well? Or do you feel the motion? Or is not that one sweet drink too much? Have you considered that a feeling of infinite sadness inside often arises from no more than an error of the table—or for that matter of the soda-fountain? Now that I come to look at you, you seem a sugar-intolerant type."

"But I'm not infinitely sad inside, Miss Curricle. It's just that sitting here sometimes I get a bit down. And it's not my stomach. I think until *I* get old too I shan't be any the worse for soft drinks nearly all the time." Mrs. Kittery paused, evidently hoping to see the severity of Miss Curricle's scrutiny relax. "And anyway I like it. This is a bonzer drink after getting in a sweat."

With much obvious kindness of heart Mr. Hoppo chuckled. "How one does perspire," he said robustly, "even at deck-quoits on a day like this!" He paused and added pleasantly, "A *what* drink?"

"Bonzer."

At the point where soda-fountain turned into bar a three-month old copy of the *Times* folded itself together.

"Ah," said a heavily cordial voice, "an Australian. Here is a capital thing!" A military eye was revealed, merrily bent on Mrs. Kittery. "And now we know why the lady would like a green sea. Her country—though beautiful, of course—is all greys and browns. Thousands of square miles of them." A military eyebrow twitched whimsically, as if flicking away the last possibility of any offence. "I was there a week. I did think it extraordinarily beautiful, I assure you. A bit uncanny, of course, and practically no game. But dashed fine."

Mrs. Kittery's eyes rounded in surprise. "Are you an artist?" she asked. "It usually takes ordinary people who come out quite a long time. To *see* it, I mean."

"Artist?" The *Times* spread itself again rapidly. "Nothing of the kind, ma'am. Steward, small whisky!"

"I was impressed," said Mr. Hoppo in a judicial voice tempered by friendly warmth, "by the towns—cities, one should really say. One didn't expect them; one had thought only of the Great Outback. In Melbourne one might almost be in—well, in Glasgow. The better parts, of course." He paused and assumed an expression which his mirror would have assured him was delightfully roguish. "But I believe my most abiding memory will be of the soap."

"I should connect soap," said Miss Curricle, "less with the Great Outback than with the Great Unwashed. Pray explain yourself."

Mr. Hoppo, if only because he was about to solicit laughter himself, giggled perfunctorily at this witticism.

"In Australia," he said, "they advertise their soap as guaranteed under the Pure Food Act. I could never observe it without mirth. The Land of the Sapophagi. Or perhaps it represents the Australians' really acting on the maxim that inner cleanliness comes first."

Mr. Hoppo giggled again. The *Times* disapprovingly crackled—less perhaps at the joke in itself than at its association with Mr. Hoppo's never wholly invisible cloth. Miss Curricle discernibly wavered between attitudes and was ambushed by a titter. And a quiet young man in a far corner thought to make the experiment of grinning cheerfully at Mrs. Kittery. In Mrs. Kittery's response, he noted, there was nothing conspiratorial. She needed no support, being as yet unaware of being obscurely conscious of offence. Indeed she now laughed suddenly and loudly, as one who sees a joke that has long been there for the seeing.

"When *I* got to Australia," said Miss Curricle, "I understood it was New Zealand. There had been a mistake. A man in an office had given me the wrong booklet. I thought the scenery was disappointing and I complained and then it *came out*. That it was Australia, that is to say. And they would make no refund. Nevertheless there were things in Australia that I liked." Miss Curricle pronounced this verdict incisively, as if conscious that she was abundantly restoring a proper tone to the conversation. "There was —let me see—yes, there was a zoo. Somewhere—in Sydney, perhaps, or Melbourne—there was really a good zoo. Almost first-class. Only some of the animals looked a little underfed."

Mrs. Kittery, the quiet young man thought, had shifted uneasily in her seat. But perhaps she was only going to negotiate for another soft drink. Perhaps—

The military person had abandoned the *Times* and was studying something in a magazine. Now he looked up at Mrs. Kittery.

"Comical colonial bear in five letters," he said.

"I beg your pardon?"

"Comical colonial bear in five letters. Begins with a *k*."

"Koala. But it's silly." Mrs. Kittery had risen.

"Silly?"

"To call a koala a comical colonial bear. It's silly and stupid."

Mrs. Kittery spoke as one who suddenly knows that it is necessary to be heard. So it was almost a scene. They stared at her uncomprehendingly, much perplexed.

"And we don't keep half-fed animals in zoos. Or eat soap or pretend to be New Zealand. We don't—"

Mr. Hoppo extended professional hands before him.

"Badinage, my dear Mrs. Kittery," he said. "A sultry morning, the tedium of our voyage—and a little badinage results. Colonel Glover was only—"

"Stuff and nonsense, sir—and be so good as to let me speak for myself." The military person had tossed down his magazine. "Badinage my foot! Counter-jumpers' talk, sir. If the lady thinks the description of this annual offensive she's entitled to say so. Remember a fellow once called a capital retriever of mine a dear dumb friend. Respect the feeling. Don't Colonel-Glover-was-only me, sir."

Mr. Hoppo squared himself in his chair. "I only proposed—"

"Ptscha!" said Colonel Glover.

Miss Curricle put her book under her arm and rose.

"I can only withdraw. One scarcely expects English gentlemen—"

"Rubbish!" said Mr. Hoppo and Colonel Glover together.

"I do think you all exceedingly odd!" said Mrs. Kittery.

"Odd!" Mr. Hoppo suddenly shouted. "And was it not you, madam, and your bear that first—"

"Moderate your voice, sir," said Colonel Glover; "moderate your voice in the presence of ladies."

"Sir," said Mr. Hoppo, "you may keep your prescriptions for your parade ground."

"Disgraceful!" said Miss Curricle, a little shrill. "Dis-*grace*-ful!"

The quiet young man sighed a quiet but—as it seemed —oddly compelling sigh. For there was a moment's silence.

And in the silence a new voice spoke from the door.

"Excuse?" it said politely.

The black man's voice. And this made it very awkward—like a scene conducted before servants but with certain imponderables added. Because the black man was not a servant; carried most easily about with him, indeed, the air of being a master on the largest scale. Had he been an Indian it would have been easier. Colonel Glover knew all about Indians—all about the proper relations with the different kinds in different places—which, after all, is all that there is to know. Colonel Glover had sometimes explained how the same Indian must not be regarded as quite the same Indian in different places: in a presidency, in a native state, on a ship going from England to India, or from India to England, or—as in this case—not from or to India at all. But about this black man Colonel Glover had confessed to not knowing the rules; Asiatics and Eurasians, he had said, were after all a considerable field in themselves and one could scarcely know about Africans too. Actually, he believed, the position was very simple— *very* simple. Still, there might be exceptions—special cases of which this conceivably was one. The First Officer—

who was Irish and probably irresponsible—had sworn the fellow possessed a diplomatic passport. The Captain declared him to be a missionary. Irreconcilable statements these, and the first extremely improbable. Though with Halifax at the F.O. one never knew. Anyway here he was, a vast creature who seemed to carry the music of tom-toms faintly about with him, pushing in to wolf a sherbet. And this scene going on.

"Excuse?" said the black man.

It is not customary to ask permission to step into a sun-deck café for a sherbet. The black man therefore was thrusting the colour problem forward. His voice, rich and grave, might proceed from a vast lake of simplicity or from a well of irony equally vast. The idiom was un-English and deliberate; the accent was Eton and apparently spontaneous. And he moved among the littered tables like a mighty hunter. Mrs. Kittery was plainly vividly aware of him. Colonel Glover coughed, attempted speech, faltered, coughed again like a faulty engine achieving a second start.

"Nice morning," he said. "But a bit on the humid side."

The black man—might he be a Zulu?—brilliantly smiled.

"I like it moist," he said—and his voice was as the Society for Pure English speaking through a magnifying and deepening machine. "Do you know where I often make for in London? The acclimatization house at the zoo."

-{ 9 }-

"The acclimatization house!" Miss Curricle was startled.

The black man bowed. "Among the gorillas," he said gravely. And taking a deep breath he raised both arms and drummed unobtrusively on his chest.

Miss Curricle involuntarily gathered her skirts about her, as if envisaging the instant necessity of dodging behind a tree.

"It must be a great change," she said vaguely. "London, I mean. After—after your part of the world."

Mr. Hoppo made a large gesture at the ocean. "Do you," he asked with cordiality, "know the Pacific well?"

The black man did not immediately reply, and they all looked out, as if some survey of the beating waters might help him to an answer. The horizon, very remote from this height, swayed rhythmically up and down, a faintly serrated line between blues. It enclosed emptiness and the ceaseless impotent friction of the waters. No one could know the Pacific, and perhaps the black man's momentary silence implied as much.

"Only a small corner," he said. "I have done some work in the Tamota group."

"Ah," said Mr. Hoppo, and his voice took on a new tone. "How wide the field! And how few—"

"I am an anthropologist."

"Indeed!" Mr. Hoppo, abandoning his professional voice, contorted his features into a fair representation of the incisiveness of the scientist. "An absorbing study, sir."

"There were some fascinating things there. They would interest you, I believe."

"I am sure of it." Mr. Hoppo spoke without certainty.

"There is one incarnation myth in particular—"

"Ah!" Mr. Hoppo began to peer about him. "I wonder where I can have left—"

"Mr. Hoppo," said Miss Curricle, "is a clergyman." She spoke with a severity which ambiguity rendered formidable. "I am a good deal interested myself—"

Mrs. Kittery interrupted. Her eyes, the quiet young man noted, had been widening upon the new-comer as he rather wished they would widen on him; now she spoke at her most eager.

"About that zoo," she asked; "that zoo in London. Would you say they feed the animals as they ought?"

"No." He was looking at her without complicity or surprise but there was a remote and understanding mischief in his voice; perhaps, the young man thought, he had an extra and primitive sense or two tucked away. "No. In point of strict diatetics it may be sound enough. But the tastes of the creatures are inadequately consulted. Take the hippopotamus: the hippopotamus must have mangoes."

"The hippopotamuses always have mangoes in Australia," said Mrs. Kittery, and paused to garner a displeased sound from Miss Curricle. "And custard-apples —is that right?" She was looking up with great innocence into the black man's eyes.

"Perfectly right," said the black man. He looked quickly at Colonel Glover, who had menacingly coughed. "In moderation, of course."

"Of course." Mrs. Kittery offered the black man potato crisps, and at this Mr. Hoppo coughed too. "Do you know," she said suddenly, "I've just thought of the title of a book?"

"Indeed?" inquired Mr. Hoppo, and made disapproving faces behind the black man's back. "It would scarcely have occurred to me that you were an authoress."

"I'm not. But sometimes I like to think of books it would be fun to write." Mrs. Kittery's remarks were now addressed with frankly wanton concentration to the black man only. "This one is the result"—she hesitated for a phrase—"of the association of ideas. Is that right?"

The black man laughed, and his laugh like his accent was at once correct and disturbingly alive.

"I can't tell," he said, "until I know the title."

"It's—" Mrs. Kittery collapsed into mirth. "It's—" She collapsed again. "It's *Mr. Hoppo's Hippo*." And she laughed the quick clear laugh of one who enjoys great simplicity of mind.

Because there would be incivility in either laughter or a stony face, the black man smiled. He smiled at the now almost contiguous Mrs. Kittery. And his smile, perhaps because it had a richness and an otherness that matched his voice, was too much for Colonel Glover. The proprieties of Poona, the convictions of Kuala-Lumpur, rose in him.

"A British lady—" he began, and paused upon finding the quiet young man planted squarely in his path.

"Quite an Imperial occasion," said the young man cheerfully. "We only want a convinced Irishman and harmony would be complete."

There was an uncertain silence.

"The sun never sets on us. So at least it can't go down upon our wrath." He laughed swiftly, rather as one draws children to laugh at nothing very much. "I think," he added inconsequently, "I see the bugler just starting on his round."

"Um," Colonel Glover looked awkwardly at his watch. "One o'clock."

"Luncheon," said Mr. Hoppo, still rather pink from digesting his hippo. "One had no idea."

Miss Curricle rose. "The sky *and* the sea," she said magnificently, "are miraculously blue."

"But I really believe"—Mr. Hoppo roguishly beamed —"that the sky has it, after all."

"No; I must admit that the sea—"

"And it's all so peaceful," said Mrs. Kittery. "Nothing, perhaps, within a hundred miles. It's all so"—she searched for an enormous word—"so inviolate."

" 'Compass'd by the inviolate sea,' " said Mr. Hoppo in the special voice of clergymen when they are making a cultural reference.

"Dear Lord Tennyson," said Miss Curricle, unconsciously quoting, perhaps, words which had impressed her nursery years.

"Peaceful," said Colonel Glover. "That's it. Utterly peaceful. We're right out of it. That's what's so strange. So out of it that one can hardly believe in it. That's what's so dashed odd."

There was a pause in which they looked at one another soberly. Then Mr. Hoppo spoke from the side. "Miss Curricle, I can see a whale."

Miss Curricle almost archly smiled. "Now, Mr. Hoppo—"

But Mr. Hoppo was frowning. "At least I *think*—"

And at this moment it happened. The ship shivered. The universe turned to a gigantic runaway lift. To that and to one vast explosion deep in the heart of which could be heard the tiny tinkle of broken cocktail glasses.

Mr. Hoppo had not seen a whale.

2

"THE WISE MEN OF GOTHAM FOUND THEMSELVES IN A not dissimilar situation." As she enunciated this Miss Curricle slithered cautiously on the plate-glass and curiously regarded the depths below. "There is nothing in sight?"

The black man, perched hazardously on the ruins of the bar, shook his head. *"Od' und leer das Meer."*

"You could scarcely have recourse to a less suitable language."

"The wise men of Gotham presumably spoke it."

"Would anyone care," Mr. Hoppo asked, "for a Gilded Lady or a Raspberry Spider?"

The sun-deck café—except that it had turned upside down—was much as it had been. But the liner of which it had formed so inconsiderable a part was gone, and—wrenched away—it floated grotesquely upon an empty ocean under an empty sky. Angry and oddly exalted, the six people left above water had established a tone which was civilized and dry. It was like a hastily rigged emotional jury-mast. Each no doubt wondered for how long it would serve.

Colonel Glover was making a tour of inspection. "One

heard some odd effects of high explosive in Spain," he said. "Fellows blown on the roofs of churches and left to cling there unharmed. That sort of thing. But nothing quite so deuced odd as this." He poked at the structure beneath him. "The frame is chrome steel and the glass inch-thick and bedded in rubber, so it's strong enough. Rides nicely, too. Trim her a bit though, with advantage. Hoppo, just shift that case of Vichy-Celestins a bit to starboard—beside Mr.—"

"Appleby," said the quiet young man.

"Appleby. Glover's my name. Lancers."

"C.I.D."

Colonel Glover blinked in the seeping sunshine. "Beg pardon?"

"A policeman."

"Bless my soul. Most unexpected. Precious little traffic to direct hereabouts, I'm afraid." Colonel Glover chuckled doubtfully and his eye searched the horizon—perhaps for social bearings. "Happen to know my nephew, Rupert Ounce?"

"He was my assistant last year."

"Ah." Glover was relieved. "Well, now we all know each other. Except—" He glanced upwards at the black man.

"Unumunu," said the black man gravely.

"Mr. Unumunu."

On a large square of plate-glass Mrs. Kittery was lying on her stomach, watching small fishes darting an inch beneath her nose. Now she turned round on her back.

"But perhaps you are a prince?" she asked.

The black man smiled brilliantly. "Once upon a time, as it happens, I was a king. And after that I was knighted. I am Sir Ponto Unumunu."

"Sir Ponto!" said Colonel Glover, startled. "I once had—" He checked himself.

"In my language Ponto means 'circumspect in battle.' It is not perhaps a very good name for a knight, who is now commonly one who has been circumspect in trade. Miss Curricle, here I think is a comfortable chair."

"Thank you, Sir Ponto."

On curves of steel, on strips of vivid red leather, Miss Curricle swayed upon the Pacific Ocean. It was calm with only the deep sea swell; the waters were like a vast big dipper, flattened out and slowed down for a wealthy cardiac patient; the sky held a blue as hard as bronze; the sun stood absolute in its heaven. The inverted dome of the café thrust down into the unknown element—a dream aquarium against which the wandering sharks and devil-fish might press curious noses, wondering at the spidery-limbed creatures within.

"Six siphons and a case of mineral water," said Mr. Hoppo, who was counting the unbroken stores. "Whisky, brandy, port, madeira, sherry—*fino*, I am glad to say—and a large number of liqueurs. An ice-box but no ice—that was what the steward, poor fellow, had gone to get a supply of. Caviar—an uncommonly big pot. A tin of biscuit-things to serve it on. Stuffed olives. Potato crisps, salted almonds, anchovies, pretzel-sticks: everything, in fact, to encourage a brisk traffic at the bar. A tin of salt, no doubt to give everything a sprinkle of from time to time. Glover, there is irony in this."

"A thing for doing the fizzing to shakes," said Mrs. Kittery, who had crossed to the debris of the soda-fountain. "It's electric, so it won't be much good." She sighed her disappointment. "A packet of straws. A flagon of vanilla flavouring, not even cracked, and a label on the back saying it's enough for forty gallons. A tub of cream, swizzle sticks, cherries, quite a lot of tinned fruit for making melbas and sundaes." Innocent satisfaction was creeping into her voice. "Ice-cream, raspberry balm, glacé pineapple—"

"Cigars," said Miss Curricle, tapping a box with her toe. She spoke gloomily, as if this further useless discovery were a luckless materialization of her own will. "And two fire-extinguishers."

"Possibly a sail." Appleby had found an inverted cupboard near a fragment of what had been the floor, and he was hauling out an enveloping sheet. "They swathed the soda-fountain with it at night. But what about a mast?"

"Up here," said Unumunu, "the teak is mostly three by three-quarters. But there's one joist three by three. If we could step it—"

"And rig that counter as a rudder," said Glover.

"With a table-leg," said Hoppo, "for tiller—"

18

APPLEBY ON ARARAT

Miss Curricle, steadying herself as the café tilted and slid down a smooth gradient of water, opened her book.

"While you are all busy with these technical things," she said, "I shall read aloud. It will be well to mention that the book is called *Tonga Trench* and is a work of scientific oceanography. Dealing as it does with the ocean-bed in certain areas of the Pacific it is of particular interest in our present situation."

The café was moving slowly skywards with the motion of an escalator; on the crest of the swell it wobbled and a flip of spray whipped them; it gave a tentative pirouette as of a ballerina waiting in the wings and slid smoothly downwards once more. The men sweated at the teak joist. Mrs. Kittery, her flawless figure everywhere touched to an innocent and plastic voluptuousness by the sun, strenuously helped. It did not look like being an easy job.

" 'Cerberus muriaticus,' " read Miss Curricle, " '*is uniquely distinguished by the possession of three distinct and separate digestive systems, with the full complement of orifices, tubes and accessory organs which this remarkable organization entails. When all three stomachs are distended—commonly by the intake of the common sea-bun or sea-kidney—the creature presents a grotesquely bulbous appearance and seems to suffer acute discomfort not unsuggestive of the purely human ailment of* mal de mer. *The eye has a more than fish-like glaze, movement is hindered by violent spasms of colic, a suggestion of* rictus *attends the gape of the jaw.'* "

Mrs. Kittery, whose eye had been wandering to the glacé pineapple, turned rather abruptly again to the mast. A complete absence of tools and the frangibility of the surfaces on which they were supported made progress slow: nevertheless it seemed likely that a mast, sufficient to support a sail filled with a light breeze, could be got up. The practical gain, Appleby reflected as he worked, would be of the slightest. Nothing could make their fantastic raft into a vessel capable of directing itself across the Straits of Dover, let alone to any goal amid this infinity of water. But the psychological use of being a little under way might be considerable; the shadow of navigation would be better than mere drift. Particularly at night, when the mind could give itself to the notion of steering by the stars.

Glover slapped the mast noisily, glanced warily at Miss Curricle—she was continuing to maintain the spirits of the company after her own fashion—and spoke in a low voice.

"Appleby—what d'you think?"

"If the ocean stays like this we're all right for several days. Then a week's coma. With luck one of us might stay intermittently conscious for a fortnight. Which wouldn't be bad."

" '*Distinct from this,*' " announced Miss Curricle, " '*is* cerberus muriaticus muricatus. *Here each lower jaw carries a sharp spear or prickle, so that the general appearance*

*is somewhat suggestive of a three-headed submarine uni-
corn.'* "

"Not bad?" said Glover—and stared at Appleby hard
but not disapprovingly.

" *'When hunting in shoals through the eerie jungle of
the ocean-bed this species gives a striking impression of
combined ferocity and efficiency. A co-operative method
has been evolved. Each individual impales three or more
sea-buns on his prickle and then proffers the refection
thus secured to its nearest companion.'* "

"Not bad in that it does give us an outside chance. On
a shipping-route—even in the Pacific—fourteen days is
something. And of course there may be a search; it depends on what the wireless people managed." Appleby's
glance went grimly to the empty sea.

" *'The reproductive mechanisms of these creatures,'* "
read Miss Curricle unflinchingly, " *'are curious in an extreme.'* "

Mrs. Kittery momentarily suspended her labours; Mr.
Hoppo gave the impression of a man who is absorbedly
humming a little tune in his head. Unumunu, who had
taken off his shirt as he worked, was ebony and immobile
by what was to be the prow. And to the west the sun sank
towards the Philippine Basin. They were alone with themselves and the nether world conjured about them by Miss
Curricle. Barren and eternally striving, its every rising
and withdrawing surface netted and embossed with veins,
flecked and fretted with foam, the ocean possessed them.

And they longed for the seaside, the approximate human thing, longed for the babble from the beach, the floating peel, the impatient hoot at the pier, the waddle or swoop of gulls. But about them there was only the momentary life of flying fish, fluid bodies half dissolved in light and, beyond, the occasional irresponsible roll of dolphins.

Cerberus muriaticus was disposed of—the data given, the senses even. The mast was up and a sail rigged; it was possible to discern that the café moved other than at the will of the waters. Mr. Hoppo talked of islands, of flying-boats, of pearl-luggers, of benevolent natives in ocean-going canoes. There were manoeuvres to provide a decent segregation of the sexes; there was an apportioning of stores and a meal which Mrs. Kittery, eating ice-cream and wafers, cheerfully called tea. The path to the sun was a foreshortened trail of fire; the orb reddened, grew, touched the horizon, and incontinently tumbled out of view in a flash of green light. Miss Curricle, providently scavenging crumbs, remarked that with one stride came the dark.

Features faded; only forms remained; there was a brief loosening of tongues.

"We *ought* to have Mr. Hoppo's hippo here," said Mrs. Kittery, with whom a joke did not readily lose its first freshness. "It would make it just like the Ark. Mr. Hoppo, do you believe in the Ark—or is it just a story?"

Miss Curricle coughed warningly, as if she felt their situation peculiarly unsuitable to theological discussion.

But Mr. Hoppo was not displeased.

"I certainly believe in the historical authenticity of Noah's Flood. But it is a story too, having been contrived by Providence with an allegorical intention."

"It seems a little hard on the poor sinners," said Unumunu; "subjecting them for the purposes of allegorical statement to the horrors of a universal deluge. But on the historical fact I agree. Almost every folk-lore contains reference to a flood. The melting of a polar ice-cap may have had something to do with it."

Mr. Hoppo could be seen to sit up, rather like a don stirred from somnolence by an unexpectedly intelligent undergraduate.

"That the immediate mechanisms involved," he said carefully, "should be explicable in what are commonly called natural or scientific terms is scarcely an argument—"

"Miss Curricle," interrupted Mrs. Kittery, for whom abstract discussion had no appeal, "shall be Noah's wife. And—and Sir Ponto is Ham."

"Mrs. Noah if you please," said Miss Curricle, somewhat heavily unbending. "If we are really like the Ark— and we could scarcely be less like a *ship*—it may be a good omen that we shall find an Ararat. And now I think that we had better go to bed." She peered about her. "Or perhaps it is necessary to use a genteelism and suggest that we *retire*."

Mr. Hoppo rummaged in the darkness. "How fortunate

that there are several rugs! I am reminded less of the Ark than of the *Swiss Family Robinson*. You remember how everything necessary turned up."

"It is overdone." Miss Curricle was decisive. "Too many visits to the wreck. I prefer *Coral Island*."

"For that matter," said Glover, "I don't think you can beat *Robinson Crusoe*. So dashed convincing . . . 'stonishing book."

"My people have many stories of the finding of islands," said Unumunu, and his voice sounded deeper with the night. "They are found after many suns, some of them —and many moons. Some are not found at all, and they are the fortunate islands—the islands of the blessed. And that is another universal legend." He sighed. "Known, Mrs. Kittery, whether where *Japhet* dwells, or *Cham*, or *Sem*."

"Once I saw a serial"—Mrs. Kittery's voice was a shade uncertain in the darkness—"and some people were wrecked and found an island . . ."

They were asleep. Strangely, quickly—except Appleby, who took first watch—they were asleep in corners of their hazardous craft. The stars blazed, an electric multitudinous fire, and Orion somersaulted towards the horizon. Cork-like the café rose and fell to the slither of the ocean. Of sound there was only a lapping; the ear, cheated and uneasy, sought the quiver, the rhythmic thud and swish of a liner's progress, the high uncanny whistle that comes into a ship's rigging below the line. They were running before a faint westerly, and conceivably making over a knot; in nine months, Appleby reflected, they might reach Peru. And learn what was left of the world. . . .

In the dark somebody softly, briefly groaned. *Each in his little bed conceived of islands* . . . He rose and lashed the tiller—work in the morning might make the steering-gear less a convention—and moved cautiously round the café. They had shipped no drop of water; the thing rode on an even keel, like some craft fantastically disguised for a regatta and overtaken by night. But in the centre of what was now the floor stood a ventilator, an affair of strong and watertight louvres. A tug at that— Appleby's fingers went over it thoughtfully, as might the fingers of others on other watches during successive nights. A tug, and much almost certainly futile suffering would be cut out, would drift down unborn amid the wheeling platoons of *cerberus muriaticus.*

He had a small torch and flashed it circumspectly. The ventilator was operated by a handle—no, not by a handle, but by a species of key, the kind that is merely a tapered bar of metal with a handle at the broader end. He tugged it out and pitched it into the sea. He moved to the bar and pitched out the whisky and the liqueurs; to the soda-fountain and pitched out the flagon of chemical stuff that would flavour forty gallons. Returning to the tiller his foot struck the box of cigars; he removed four and threw away the box. The policeman's instinct, he thought to himself, and lighting his own cigar sat down again at his post. Scraps of verse ran in his head. *To be or not to be. To lie in cold obstruction and to rot. If I drink oblivion of a day so shorten I the stature of my soul. But need'st not strive officiously to keep alive.* . . . He drew at the cigar—a good cigar, with its place in that hierarchy of desirable sensations which makes man inescapably desirous to fulfil his day and to draw out the night of age. He looked up at the stars. They had nothing to say, but they were undoubtedly pretty and it was easy to feel that they were majestic and mysterious. He looked out over the darkness of the ocean. Too much infinity doesn't do. He fell to thinking of the situation in Turkey. There were interesting possibilities there.

3

THE SUN NOW TOOK LONGER—AT LEAST TWICE AS LONG
—to circle the heavens, and its beams were hotter—at
least twice as hot. The rugs were rigged to give sluggishly
drifting parallelograms of shade. Under one Hoppo knelt
in prayer. And they were embarrassed—all except Mrs.
Kittery, who had never come across the thing before,
and who watched with her blue and black lips parted in
innocent interest. She was still physically splendid,
Appleby thought. Like a better quality linoleum, that
wears the same all through. But there was not much wear
left even in Mrs. Kittery.

The café swooped down a lengthening glissade of
water; something was going to happen to the weather.
Hoppo rolled over and over like a half-filled sack of
potatoes and came up against Glover at the tiller.

"I feel myself," he whispered, "getting higher and
higher."

"Higher?" Glover looked up at the menacing line of
water above them.

"My position. I have been reconsidering the Thirty-
nine Articles."

"Thirty-nine fathoms," said Miss Curricle. "Forty

fathoms. Forty-one fathoms."

Miss Curricle had gone out of her mind some days before and had been deep in the Tonga Trench ever since. It appeared, from what she reported, to be cool and dark—the darkness however relieved by streams and whorls and gyres of brilliantly illuminated fish. Some were dim masses with a single piercing searchlight in the brow; some, like a circus-tent at night, were outlined in beads of coloured fire; some were a single translucent glow. A Piccadilly Circus world of the not so long ago. And a predatory world. Miss Curricle swayed her body and one knew that she had again dodged the snap of cavernous jaws, the writhe and swoop of tenacles ten feet long.

To Appleby at the prow Unumunu in the ghost of Unumunu's voice whispered ceaseless anthropology. The Kipiti, the Aruntas, the Papitino, the Tongs. Phantasmagorically the café drifted over mango swamps, across deserts and tundras, beneath eucalypts and palms. Internecine islands hovered on the horizon, thickened to archipelagoes where the narrow seas were stained with blood. Assagais fell from the sun and the faint wind held the rhythm of drums, chants to unknown modes, tread of feet in ritual dance.

(The tips of the swell, as if at the burgeoning of a fantastic Spring, were here and there flecked or streaked with foam; Glover sat like eroded granite at the tiller.)

The Kola Islanders worship clouds, in the Luba Group people don't know why babies come, the god of the

Arrimattaroa is a gigantic termite. It was all enormously
interesting, Unumunu whispered. Scientifically interesting. He spoke of institutes, endowments, expeditions; of
monographs and museums. One never knew where one
would get to—the fascination to a man of science like
himself was there. The most fantastic rite, the most re-
pellent custom might yield on study the basis for some
masterful generalization, some far-reaching and revolu-
tionary anthropological theory.

(The sun went down with its green flash and then—as
if pleased with this trite effect—did it again. There was
no one at the tiller; there was no tiller; the sail was a
tattered gonfalon merely; the air was hot, still and dry,
but there was a whisper in it, a moan behind the horizon.)

Sprawled under his rug Hoppo no longer prayed; days
ago he had conversed on the Thirty-nine Articles with
the Seraphic Doctor and been rocketed higher than ever,
so that he had further fascinated Mrs. Kittery by announcing the performance of meditations on the Splendid Bride
and the Nine Sacred Cataracts. And now, herself with
the strength of the Seraphim, Mrs. Kittery was hauling
him by the heels—hauling at his heels because the sun
was there again and his head must have shade or seethe.

Appleby had ruled for a time, but now Mrs. Kittery
did that. She alone remained of the normal world—a normal woman fighting for life in a normal hazard of war.
And among them she had the superior reality, the superior
physical actuality, of a Homeric goddess. Miss Curricle's

hair was a ghost-coral and her limbs uncertainly waved; she was insubstantial to the point of losing a dimension, as if the incalculable pressures of a hundred fathoms had dealt with her like a hydraulic press. Glover was an obliterated monolithic figure, mysteriously upright but human or alive in nothing else; Hoppo was as shrunken as a Skin of Bartholomew; Unumunu was only a voice, now weirdly chanting, now desperately whispering anthropology still. But Mrs. Kittery remained and ruled; five people were to be kept alive and she would hold down the job. She wound her watch and waited for the hour hand to circle twice before opening the last tin of pears.

Unumunu stopped chanting; an ebony cloud hovered before Appleby; the voice was at his ear.

"Or take the whole theory of the transference of strength. Primitive peoples are in nothing more interesting—more interesting to the scientist—than in that. . . . What is your name?"

"Appleby—John Appleby."

"There—you have given yourself away! Literally, Mr. Appleby, I have your name and your name is *you*. I have you in my power. I have *your* power. Along with your name I have received it into myself. You see? It is a universal and most potent magic." The voice paused, and then went hurriedly on. "Most interesting. It has been studied by Berthold and Kemp-Brown. By Oplitz among the Kagotas . . . work on the Guggenberg Foundation . . . the Poincet-Conti Expedition." The voice paused again. "And cannibalism," it said, "is much the same sort of thing."

(The Pacific Ocean had become very still. The dip and climb of the café was now only a delusion of the semi-circular canals; instead it spun like a dying roulette-wheel, like an infinitely lazy top. The café spun slower, slower yet, there was an instant of absolute motionlessness, it was spinning with faintly gathering momentum in reverse. A barometer, had there been one on board, would have been in process of registering a sensational drop. Perhaps it grew a shade cooler; perhaps because of this Appleby opened his eyes.)

Appleby opened his eyes and saw a Sir Ponto Unumunu who was no longer talking anthropology. Instead, he was advancing painfully upon Mrs. Kittery. In his hand he held a fair-sized penknife, open at the larger blade.

The situation was clear. If there was strength to be magically acquired in the shape of a reasonably succulent collop, it was from Mrs. Kittery that it must come. Appleby made a very great effort to call out. A noise of sorts must have resulted, because Mrs. Kittery turned round. The black man, though quite nearly dead, was still a beautifully sprung and jointed machine; Mrs. Kittery looked at him at once with disapproval and with continued frank sensuous enjoyment. He jumped at her. And she stepped out of the way and hit him hard on the head with a bottle.

In the instant that Mrs. Kittery hit Unumunu the storm

hit the café. It ruined any dramatic effect that a little attempted man-eating might have had. The café spun madly, so that they were all flung to its periphery; then it bounded forward so that they tumbled in a common heap. A great demon was overhead, yelling as if tortured by a demon greater still; prowling the ocean about them were forces not conceivable even in demoniac terms. And it was suddenly dark—dark with a darkness the more intimidating because it was perhaps the issue only of senses supremely confused. The café veered and there was audible above the scream of the storm an ominous crack; veered again and seemed to plunge outright from the torrid to a frigid zone. They were soaked and chilled—but it was water from the heavens and not from an engulfing sea. Mysteriously impelled, the café raced as if on the brink of Niagara, as if plunging into that final vortex of the earth's waters imagined by Poe. The café raced, the storm yelled and the humans, revived, yelled too—like airmen power-diving to their physical limit. Appleby yelled once and would have yelled again, but the mast came down and hit him much as the bottle had hit Unumunu. He saw, in a queer flash of extended awareness, Miss Curricle, very sane, looking up as if in gloomy collaboration with heaven. And then he tumbled to the glassy floor.

4

COMMONLY ONE EMERGES FROM A FAINT OR AN ANAES-
thetic into a world of massive and confused sights and
sounds—or into a mélange or continuum of these from
which the normal boundaries of the senses presently dis-
engage themselves. But Appleby came to entirely in terms
of his nose.

The universe consisted of a smell of earth—slightly
dank, slightly lush, but splitting upon exploration into a
magnificent multitudinousness, into a nasal splendour as
of light cast through a spectroscope. Infinite beckoning
labyrinths of scent, like a first-class grocer's before Christ-
mas. *Sabean* Odours from the spicie shoare of *Arabic* the
blest. Fruits of pomegranate and peach. And all divinely
new, like a first bringing of the powers of manhood into
play. The innocent nose . . . Appleby half sat up.

Appleby half sat up and the movement brought him
into a fresh olfactory stratum. There was a smell of
charred aromatic wood; there was a further smell so
primitive that it prickled at the roots of his hair and laid
invisible fingers on his spine. Like roast pork. For a moment the universe contracted to a clamant square inch at
the root of his tongue.

He opened his eyes, or perhaps looked through eyes that were already open. And he saw Unumunu, ebon, vast, anointed, bare to the waist, turning a shapeless lump of flesh on a spit. The fingers on Appleby's spine closed like a vice; his eye-balls refused their motion, transfixed on this sight; his memory worked. . . . And then he painfully turned his whole head and saw Mrs. Kittery, placidly seated in a Tahitian attitude on the farther side of a fire.

Unumunu twisted his torso with a musculature remote as the Congo; spoke in a voice familiar as Isis or the Cam.

"You are all right now, Appleby, my dear fellow? I gather the mast hit us both on the head."

"It was dreadful," said Mrs. Kittery, large-eyed and ardent. "Mr. Hoppo insisted on administering the supreme junction." She had a gourd in her lap and was sucking some pleasingly saccharine beverage through a cane.

"The supreme junction?" Appleby got painfully to his knees. "Where are we now?"

Unumunu's teeth gleamed. "Not in Paradise—unless of the terrestrial sort. This is what the songs celebrate as a tropic isle."

"There are yams," breathed Mrs. Kittery, "and coconuts and you can make a house of bamboos. You can—you can wear a sarong."

"Have some toasted terrapin."

"You can rub in coconut oil and go absolutely brown."

Appleby ate terrapin cautiously and became for a time

absorbed in an astounding consciousness of his metabolic processes. It was like being a hysterical subject and seeing one's own inside.

"Are we the only survivors?" he asked presently.

"Oh, no!" Mrs. Kittery was slightly shocked. "There's Miss Curricle, of course. She's gone for a bathe round the point."

"And Glover and Hoppo," said Unumunu, "have gone for a walk. It seems that the Colonel has Anglo-Catholic tendencies and Hoppo is expostulating from the Low Church standpoint. On a mundane level they are looking for eggs."

"—For dinner," added Mrs. Kittery. "The Colonel says that now we are properly settled we had better dine at eight. That"—she pointed to the terrapin—"is the end of lunch. And this"—she held up the gourd—"is afternoon tea—I mean, is tea." She sucked again.

Appleby felt a new dazedness come over his sense. It was so difficult to catch up.

"Is the island, then, uninhabited?" he asked.

Unumunu nodded regretfully. "I am afraid so—although there are still parts to explore. What an opportunity for field-work lost! Think if we had hit upon a matriarchy, or a new clan system! The Guggenberg Foundation—"

The terrapin was stowed; Appleby closed his eyes, and with them his ears closed too. When he awoke it was to find his companions vanished and only the remains of the fire to assure him he had not been dreaming. Perhaps Mrs. Kittery was applying coconut oil; perhaps Unumunu was hopefully seeking some Man Friday's footstep in the sand. He got to his feet and found his legs by no means shaky; he strolled about and examined his environment.

It was exotic enough, a subtropical confusion tumbling to a sickle of beach with calm sea and a reef beyond. No doubt there were yams. Perhaps there would be mammee and manchineel and mangosteen as well. But compared with the nightmarish absurdity of the sun-deck café the place was as comfortingly commonplace as could be. Appleby, though without any taste—or talent, maybe—for a South Sea Idyll, looked about him with moderate approval. As Mrs. Kittery had remarked, one could construct a shelter of bamboos. There was terrapin and fruit and—apparently—water. They commanded fire. It was not a rainy season. They had only accident, disease and each other to reckon with—and perhaps a steamer would turn up one day.

He descended to the beach and looked out to sea. There was a shark in the lagoon—impossible to mistake that triangular fin. On the reef beyond, and silhouetted against the dazzle of the declining sun, were two curved and sickly palms; their effect was as of home-made decorations in a forlorn-hope teashop; Appleby surveyed them and felt no stirring of romance. But beyond them and beyond the farthest strip of ocean something was happening. For a moment it looked like a ship coming hull-up on the horizon; then it rose a fraction into air, like Gulliver's floating island. And an island it was—or perhaps the tip of a continent—miraging up from an indeterminable distance beyond the curve of earth. Appleby stared at it, absorbed. Perhaps one could really actualize some school-boys' yarn; perhaps one could make tools with which to make tools to make—

A voice spoke behind him. "Evening on Ararat," it said.

He turned round and saw Miss Curricle. A woman who has plumbed the Tonga Trench ought to be older for the experience—but Miss Curricle, he saw at once, looked younger than before. Perhaps it was her clothes; these, originally conceived on angular lines, had been collapsed by the sea and now conformed approximately to the contours beneath. One was aware, Appleby saw with vague foreboding, that Miss Curricle belonged to the same order of beings as Mrs. Kittery. A superior policeman must have the instinct of experiment.

"Ararat?" he said. "Mrs. Kittery thinks of it rather as Eden. And I believe she is going to wear a sarong."

Miss Curricle non-committally smiled—something of a Gioconda smile that might be as good as a sarong itself if one were in the mood. Appleby was not in the mood.

"I'm afraid," he continued with a suggestion of haste, "that we may be here for some time."

"Evening on Ararat." Miss Curricle repeated her words with a faint proprietorship in the tone; she might have been standing beside a myriorama, prepared to flick a switch and offer Morning on Mont Blanc instead. "The thought has implications." She looked, darkling, at the ocean. "Has it occurred to you, Mr. Appleby, that this may be a *second* Ararat?"

"No. I fear I haven't got a theological mind."

Miss Curricle gave what, but for her new character of Inscrutable Woman, would have been a snort.

"Figuratively, of course. Noah and his family on Ararat were the only people left alive on earth. As things go, it might be approximately the same with us."

Appleby smiled. "I see what you mean. But I should be inclined to put the emphasis on approximately, all the same. They can't quite exterminate each other."

"You ought," said Miss Curricle very solemnly, "to read H. G. Wells."

"Perhaps. But I'm not likely to have the opportunity for some time. As I say, we're likely to be here for a good bit."

Miss Curricle shook her head, disapproving of the levity. "Certainly we may be here for a good bit—and as the only representatives of our species left on the planet. We may be here until there is another convulsion and some land bridge rises to lead us again into the world."

"Really, unless we have Methuselah among our number as well as Noah I hardly think—"

"I am speaking of our descendants," said Miss Curricle.

APPLEBY ON ARARAT

They turned round and in silence walked back across a beach which might have led to Lilliput, so tiny were the inconceivable myriads of whorled shells of which it was composed. They stepped off the beach and Lilliput gave way to Brobdingnag, to giant palms and arcadings of tree-fern, to yuccas thrusting up like the spears of careless giants in ambush, to a lustre of convolvulus impossibly vivid and impossibly large. Grass parrots fussed before them; there were slithers in the undergrowth and the plop of some creature taking to a pool; a goanna preened a belligerent ruff as they passed and a sleepy lizard drowsed across a log, like a lazy emissary from the world of some tropical Beatrix Potter.

"And here we are." Miss Curricle spoke as one who turns a latch-key and invites a friend to enter. They had reached a glade in which the grass would have been a sheet of emerald were it not strewn thick with a profusion of purple petals from the branches of vast and circumambient jacaranda.

It was the present headquarters of the party. Colonel Glover, who now combined military eyebrows with a nautical beard, was building a fire-place. He looked up as Appleby approached.

"Glad to see you right again. Something to talk about in a minute—official matter." He returned to the complicated arrangement of a circle of stones.

Mr. Hoppo appeared, pink under a load of bracken.

"My dear sir, I am rejoiced to see you; it is capital that we are all safe and in our right mind." He gave something between a giggle and a cough, and it was to be guessed that his conversations with the Seraphic Doctor were not to be alluded to again. "The climate looks as if it is going to be ideal." He dumped down the bracken. "Which is just as well. Our sleeping arrangements are bound to be somewhat primitive at first."

Appleby glanced at Miss Curricle—resolute to replenish the earth—and wondered if this was not rather what they were likely to be later on.

"The bracken looks very comfortable," he said. "I wonder if there are snakes?"

"Unumunu has already killed one. He declares that he found it close to Mrs. Kittery while she was plucking fruit—a species of apple, I understand—this afternoon." Mr. Hoppo gave what was definitely a latitudinarian chuckle. It looked as if he were touching what the stock-exchange calls a new low. "And now he is showing her how to set snares for pigeons." He looked vaguely round the glade. "At least that is what I understood."

There was a silence that was expressive. Glover banged stone upon stone. Hoppo looked dawningly disturbed. And then Miss Curricle spoke.

"The island," she said tartly and with satisfaction, "is not a London park. There is nobody to clatter a bell at dusk and bawl 'All out.' And it would be childish to continue to think in terms of that sort of thing. At the moment I suggest that we think of dinner instead. Careful thought must be given to diet. At present we are so many city-bred weeds. And we must grow strong." As she uttered this Tarzan-like sentiment Miss Curricle stooped with a sudden grace not at all suggestive of weediness and began to gather sticks.

It was dusk. Hoppo was looking at his piles of bracken as if in sudden doubt or discouragement; Glover was banging down his final stone. And from the mysterious world beyond the glade there came voices, a sudden laughter, a snapping of boughs. Unumunu and Mrs. Kittery appeared, their proportions momentarily heroic in the half-light.

"Pigeons," called Mrs. Kittery. "Six of them!"

"And clay." Unumunu's voice held all the texture of the advancing night. "You will find them delicious baked in clay. Colonel, light your fire."

They gathered round the flame; it leapt and was an instantaneous spell, a focus in the exactest sense.

"The flame," said Miss Curricle, "is wonderfully golden."

"Not so golden as the brand beneath," said Hoppo.

"No, not so golden as the brand."

"If only it smelt of gum leaves," said Mrs. Kittery, "and we could have billy-tea. There's nothing so nice as that."

"It must be delicious." Glover spoke unreservedly. "You must tell us about Australia; I had only a glimpse of it."

"You would love it. And it might love you."

Glover, throwing sticks on the fire, laughed pleasantly. "Well, we're one family, after all." He stopped, frowned. "That reminds me—I suppose everybody here is a British subject by birth?" He gave his companions something of a parade-ground glance. "Very well. Appleby, would you say anyone is likely to have landed here before?"

"Conceivably not. There is no sign of anything of the sort."

"Exactly. Well now, I think we ought to anex the island —just in case. Might come in handy one day. Air-bases— that sort of thing. You never can tell."

"Particularly," said Unumunu, "as we haven't the faintest idea where it is."

"Just so." Glover nodded acknowledgment of this strengthening of his argument. "Tomorrow morning, then, we'll run up a bit of a flag. And—yes—I think there ought to be a short proclamation. Some formality will be proper. After all—King's name." He paused, embarrassed.

Mrs. Kittery, vastly impressed, set down her pigeon to clap her hands.

"And shall you be Governor? And Miss Curricle lay the foundation-stone of Government House here by the fire-place?"

"Who," asked Miss Curricle, "is going to read the proclamation?"

"Well, I rather feel that Sir Ponto"—Glover enunciated the name with a shade of difficulty—"is the man. He must be regarded as taking precedence here."

"Not at all." Unumunu, upon whom the fire-light was weirdly reflected in licking tongues of flame, shook his head decidedly. "In my part of the empire, I assure you, the knights come just after the second-class clerks. So there can be no doubt at all. This important ceremony must be performed by the Colonel himself."

"Well," said Glover, "in that case—and if you all agree —perhaps after all it might be as well. Something very simple, you know. *I, Herbert Glover, a colonel of horse in His Majesty's commission—*"

Mrs. Kittery leant forward into the full light of the fire.

"I think it should be Sir Ponto." She spoke with child-like candour and equally childlike decision. "And for Governor as well."

The magic of the fire was troubled; the silence hung baffled and awkward. Then Appleby spoke.

"Perhaps it would be as well if we asked Mr. Hoppo." He cast rapidly about in his mind for supporting argument. "It would give the ceremony a certain character. Just a few simple words and—er—a short prayer."

"Or I wouldn't mind Mr. Appleby." Mrs. Kittery spoke as if she had just discovered this. "I wouldn't mind Mr. Appleby at all."

Miss Curricle rose to her feet. "This," she said, "is scarcely the real problem that confronts us. . . . Or perhaps it is."

5

Appleby and Diana Kittery lay on a rock and the sea splashed them.

"I think," she said, "that you and Ponto will kill the Colonel and poor old Hoppo."

"Surely not." He turned on his side and surveyed her perfections with a glance which was becoming increasingly dutiful merely. The Island Idyll was dreadfully boring.

"Yes. Or perhaps just enslave them." She wriggled on her stomach and kicked her heels in air at this amendment. "They could be kept to do the washing-up."

"There is no washing-up."

"They could chop wood and carry water—like Billycan in the play."

"Caliban, Diana—Caliban. But aren't you afraid that the black man might kill me too—and guzzle you up in the end? You wouldn't always have a bottle handy."

Diana trailed a brown arm luxuriously in water. "That was an awful thrill. I felt good. The whole thing was good in its horrid way. It was"—she searched for her conception—"full-time."

He burst out laughing. "There—you're bored too. Born

with the equipment of a houri, and labouring hard at the role—"

"What," she asked dangerously, "is a houri? Something not nice?"

"Not at all. It's a black-eyed girl. Born—"

"My eyes aren't black. You *know* they're not."

"Born as you are, and working to perfect the idea, you are yet enormously bored just for lack of a few honest jobs. Hoovering the carpets, perhaps, and tinkering with sherbets in the refrigerator. And the washing on Monday."

"I think you have a—a banal mind."

"Diana, where do you get these words? And, anyway, it is banal to imagine that I should do in the Colonel for a chit like you—entirely pleasing though you are in your way. We have nothing to do on this damned island, and so we turn our minds into cinemas and imagine dramatic absurdities."

"Nothing to do? There's still the exploring."

"We've been everywhere except over the east range—and that can conceal nothing but a few small coves."

"Coves?" said Diana hopefully.

"Alas, my dear—not that sort of coves. Not men. Small bays."

"Small boys?" She had an uncertain ear for strange accents, and looked bewildered.

"You are unnecessarily and enormously stupid." He jumped into the sea. "Or rather, you're not. You put it on—like the coconut oil. Actually you are a woman of astounding character. Our wanderings witnessed it. Come in."

They swam to another rock, peering down at the exotic drama clearly visible on the sea floor.

"You should have been a pair of ragged claws," he said as they climbed out.

"What?"

"Nothing—only poetry."

"It didn't *sound* like poetry. Was that Ponto across the lagoon?"

"I didn't notice. I'm not all eyes for Unumunu."

"You're horrid. I don't care a bit for Ponto today." She stretched herself. "Or rather I do. Listen. If the Colonel should die—"

"He won't."

"If the Colonel should die—preferably doing something helpful, like Masterman Ready, so that he would be happy about it—and then if we could get Hoppo *up* a bit—"

"Up a bit?"

"You know—higher again, so that he would believe in a celebrate clergy—"

"Celibate, Diana."

"That's what I said. Well then, it would be alright—wouldn't it?"

"Neither alright nor *all right*."

"John Appleby, if I didn't think it might just give you pleasure I would *bite*. And it *would* be alright. Hoppo could marry Ponto and me, and the Curricle and you—or the other way round—and nobody could say anything."

"There's nobody to say anything in any case, except a dubious entity, of unknown staying-power, called the super-ego."

"There!" Diana Kittery stared at him with her lucid and disconcerting intelligence. "I don't know what you mean. But I think you're agreeing with me. About the maddened men killing each other."

He shook his head, smiling. "Come again, in six months, and when we're having a rainy season. Then, perhaps. At present the super-ego is unchallenged. Not all your genius for flirtation, nor Miss Curricle's sense of responsibility to the species, nor yet the glamour of that great black piano appassionato—"

"That what?"

He sighed. "Just a very allusive way of referring to Unumunu. Such ingenuity shows I'm running to seed. For I'm a policeman, you know. I hunt burglars and murderers."

She looked at him round-eyed. "And spies?"

"And spies. Until I am bundled across the world to help organize a back-of-beyond C.I.D. And now this—shipwreck and the tangles of Neaera's hair. Don't you think I would relish the appearance of your absurd maddened men? I've known a good homicide give me something to bite on for weeks. Whereas, my dear, *you*—"

"I think," she said, "you must be like so many of the

English now-a-days—hankering after being the American version of the same thing."

He stood up. "You are a demon. I could believe you capable of anything."

"I could beat any homicide you've tackled. I could." She had sprung up too, brown and gold. "I could take you and run you for years, John Appleby." She became a flashing arc and vanished.

He hitched decorously at his pants and dived too—a sound but inferior performance. The setting was all hers and perhaps she was right; with sun and sea and beach about, she commanded invisible armies and could possibly have it all her own way. Or at least here he was, diving as instinctively as a bull seal after a favourite cow. . . . He rose to the surface and rebelled.

"I wish," he said to the appalling emptiness about them, "this was all different. I wish the story would take a quirk, the key change, the canvas grow."

Diana's laugh, ringing from the unexpected quarter to which she had swum under water, mocked his prayer.

"I'll race you," she called out, "right across the bay. Go!"

The idea had come to her, characteristically, because she saw she would have a start; and as she spoke she was off at a spectacular crawl. Reduced to the same deplorable mental level, he gave a moment to estimating whether he could win, and then swam powerfully after her. The water was warm and limpid, deep, but—they had dis-

covered—locked by shallows from the hazards of the
main lagoon. So one could just swim straight ahead and
hope to avoid the two kinds of jelly-fish: those that stung
and those that gave a mild electric shock. There was no
danger—

"John, go back! *Shark!*"

He felt a stab of horrible fear; it must be true, for this
was the one fool trick she would not play. He plunged
ahead. And then her voice came again. "It's O.K.! It's
stranded! And it's not a shark; it's a porpoise—a stranded
porpoise!" She was as absurd, as eagerly exclamatory, as
a child who has found a dead cat. "John, do come on!"

He swam forward vigorously. Heroism was off and the
idyll on again; the shark had evaporated and the siren
grown more alluring from the shock.

"All right," he called—and added, as automatically one
does to the very young, "don't touch it till I come."

Just ahead now the water was eddying over some barely
submerged rock; he saw the black oily curve of the creature half awash. Gulls rose in air and sharply broke the
silence with their cries; a shoal of tiny, long-snouted fishes
flashed by his nose. He raised himself in the water. The
sheen of the stranded porpoise was beautiful in the sun-
light. And somewhere—recently—he had seen it before.
He caught his breath. It was Unumunu's body that lay
sprawled on the rock. The sea lapped lazily over the
thighs, covered the head. Only the torso was exposed.
The black man was dead.

Another shoal of fish flashed past, swerving with the precision of an automobile in knock-about comedy. Somewhere on the island a kookaburra cackled; another and another took up the sound; the air was filled with a brief and diabolic laughter which ebbed to a silence in which there was only heard the faint slap of the water against the dead man's flanks.

"Diana, it's Unumunu; he's drowned. Go ashore and I'll try to bring him in."

But she was swimming forward still, although she must have realized the truth before he spoke. Now she turned round and trod water; she was pale and opened her lips cautiously, as if doubting what would emerge.

"I'll help." She tossed water from her hair and the sound of her voice seemed to give her confidence. "It's difficult, a body. Even if it's well gassed-up." She was groping for a foothold on the submerged rock.

For Appleby a dead man was scarcely an event, and he was still chiefly interested in the girl. So this, perhaps, was the Song the Sirens sang—bodies well gassed-up being a natural region of their singing.

"Don't get worried," he said by way of discounting his thoughts. "And if we go one on each side—"

"No." Whether worried or not, Diana abruptly took command. And her instructions were efficient in the extreme; they had the body and were making headway towards the shore.

A current caught them momentarily and Appleby had

a first glimpse of Unumunu's face. The sight hurried him into speech.

"You seem to know about it," he said.

"John?" She turned her head, startled.

"Handling a body in water."

"Too right. I mean, yes. We have lots of this on our beach. And I've belonged to the life-savers for years. It's great fun." She paused, perhaps feeling this an inappropriate truth, perhaps because the current, catching them again, made it necessary to conserve her breath. "But I never thought it would come to bringing in poor old Ponto." She twisted round to look at the black man's face with the innocent interest of a child examining a dead canary.

"*John!*"

"Yes."

They got the body to the beach and laid it on its back; they dropped down exhausted beside it. And Appleby looked again. Unumunu's face would soon be dust. But now it looked like something utterly permanent, like a piece of sculpture that would have great value in a museum, like the effigy of a divine being infinitely remote in the primitive consciousness of mankind. Such things are brought from the Gold Coast, from the Congo, and they rebuke every hope, negate every category of the Western mind. The dead Sir Ponto, with Eton and anthropology evaporated from his clay and his eyes open without expectation on the sky, looked like that. And the effect of sculptural fragment was increased because he had no back to his head. The back of his head had been bashed in.

"Has he been dead long? I *thought* I saw him, you know, across the lagoon." Diana's wondering eyes travelled the length of the ebony body. "The fish have been nibbling his toes." She stopped, her eyes widened. "So if *he* had nibbled *me*—" Abruptly she sat up and began to cry. She cried for a long time, while Appleby stared at the sea. "I think," she said obscurely, "he was jolly decent. Considering he was a black."

The idyll was over; the fantasy—in which she was to marry a black and he was to marry the Curricle—was broken; the story had taken its quirk and the key was changed. He stood up.

"We must find the others."

She nodded. And then her eyebrows puckered, as if she were attempting some elementary sum.

"Then it must—" She checked herself. "Could he have *fallen?*" she almost whispered.

"From a great height, yes. But there is no great height from which a body could end up in the lagoon."

"Then—"

"Yes. Come along."

6

THEY STEPPED OFF THE BEACH AND INTO THEIR NOW familiar miniature jungle—another world which made what was behind them unbelievable at once. The bowery loneliness was like Eden, Appleby thought—and like the second Eden of our infancy was the determined innocence that trod by his side. Or rather that had just left it— for Diana had suddenly darted into the undergrowth and disappeared. Perhaps he should arrest her and everybody else; perhaps he should have affected to find Unumunu's death explicable by natural means and bided his time. . . .

She was back again, tears and triumph on her face and in her hands a pigeon. "Ponto's," she said. "He *was* so good at all that." She sniffed and felt for a handkerchief which had disappeared long ago. "We shall never get along without him." She felt at the bird. "A nice plump one too. Let's keep it for ourselves."

He laughed. She looked at him reproachfully.

"John, you shouldn't laugh. Not after such a dreadful thing. Not even if you *are* a policeman—you're not really, are you?"

"Of course I am. And a puzzled one."

"Puzzled?" Her look now had its quick intelligence.

"Well, *I* don't believe it. It's not believable. That one of them, I mean—"

"But, Diana, only an hour ago you were making up just such an improbability."

"No. I never said"—she hesitated, plunged—"that Hoppo or the Colonel would or could kill anybody. I said one of—of you two might. *They're* not maddened men."

"Haven't I sufficiently impressed upon you that *I* am not a maddened man?"

"Yes, you are—in a way. And Ponto too. But the other two just don't *attend*. I ought to know, oughtn't I?"

"You think Unumunu attended? Have you ever heard of the Hottentot Venus?"

"No." Diana looked suspicious.

"She is exceedingly unlike you. And Unumunu I should judge to have had rather strict ideas, really. A little make-believe, of course. But fundamentally you would be—well, beneath his dignity. He wasn't a coloured boxer." Appleby frowned thoughtfully. "I hope," he added somewhat absent-mindedly, "you're not offended by my putting it that way?"

"Well, I've never been called a coloured boxer's type before. But if Ponto wasn't a maddened man, it seems to leave just *you*. Because *certainly* Hoppo and the Colonel don't count."

"I said I was puzzled, didn't I? But I see possibilities. Why not a maddened woman?" He paused and looked at her gravely. "Or why not a soldier or a clergyman not maddened at all, but with something quite different in his head?"

"I don't think you at all believe what you're saying."

Appleby smiled. "Perhaps you should be a policeman too. Very well, then. A maddened man, as you insist. And why should Hoppo and Glover not count? Very inhibited people—"

"What?"

"Very restrained and shy and anxiously correct people are often dippier than others. And our circumstances here are very strange and likely to call up the primitive. Perhaps it really has been called up a little quicker than I expected. Look at Miss Curricle; it was bubbling in her from the first. And it may very well be that Hoppo or Glover has gone—to a civilized mind—quietly off his head. Kill the males and possess the females. It's at once absurd, shocking, and possible."

"Nonsense." Diana was plucking the pigeon as she walked, so that she had the appearance of engaging in some leisurely paper-chase. "It's all nonsense." She spoke with a largeness and a decisiveness against which logic and consistency had no chance. "Why, Hoppo and the Colonel—" Abruptly she stopped and laid a hand on his arm. "Look. Listen."

They had reached the edge of the glade which was still their living quarters, and through a screen of hibiscus could see what was happening within. Hoppo and Glover were sitting side by side on a fallen tree-trunk; Hoppo was opening oysters and Glover was washing yams. It was a domestic scene—nor was the conversation which could be overheard of a dramatic character.

"I think I may claim," Hoppo was saying, "that I have a very devotional interior." He peered inquiringly into a dubious oyster. "Devotional and, at the same time, comfortable too."

"It was pretty certain, then"—Glover scraped at a yam with a razor shell—"that the tribes were out. That night I ordered up the seven-pounders."

"Though not a stone of the fabric, mark you, dates from before the Reformation."

"We had four pom-poms—"

"The west front is by Butterfield."

"—a howitzer badly in need of overhaul—"

"Some really nice modern glass—"

"—and a machine-gun—a new-fangled thing in which, naturally, one didn't believe."

"—wonderfully *realistic* snow. The shepherds are in blue—"

"—yelling like devils."

"There is a scroll above; it says simply *Peace on Earth*."

"—gave them a whiff of shrapnel . . ."

Diana put an arm round Appleby and gave his ribs an unexpected and vigorous squeeze.

"There!" she whispered. "You see? They don't even attend to each other any longer. It's just like people in Čapek."

He stared at her, perplexed. Here in the green shade her flesh, golden-brown as impossible toast on a hoarding, held half-lights like old bronze.

"Diana, one day you will get right in the target area. Chekov, perhaps. What makes you so literary? I suppose you enjoyed the Australian higher education?"

She looked at him suspiciously. "I took out some classes," she said briefly. "Come on."

They broke cover and advanced across the glade. Light crackled on them from a high and burning sun; the purple jacaranda-carpet shimmered and seemed to breathe; invisible crickets chirmed like an army of power-looms far away. Appleby walked up to the two men.

"Unumunu has been murdered," he said.

Their arms and their jaws dropped as if they had been idle derricks; they stared at him blankly and he stared at them hard. It occurred to him that this was something to which he had never been moved before; during all their adventures it had not happened that he had given them a searching glance. And this was discouraging. For his world had long been divided into palpable sheep and potential goats, and it was to the goats that he had developed the habit of attending.

"Murdered?" said Glover. "Good Gad!"

"Murdered?" said Hoppo. "Heaven forfend!"

They were men, surely, as simply faithful to their sort as the creations of Peter Arno. The inner life, the stifled fear, the secret lust, the *libido*, the *id*, the complex and the neurosis—these were all conceptions that wilted and failed before their absolute fidelity to the simplest of the laws of kind. The large-eyed, toast-golden Diana, who had taken out classes and who trod the island like a child, was a monster of complexity, was a fathomless well compared with these. Appleby contemplated them with a hopelessness which he tried to hope was premature.

Hoppo stood up in agitation. "Have you seen a canoe? Is there any sign of the savages?"

And Glover stood up as a man for whom the gong has sounded. "A raider! Or perhaps another part of the island is used for basing submarines. With luck we might give them a surprise. Killed—poor chap! A fine type. Magnificent fighters, you know—broke a British square or two in the old days did his sort. Rather a sophisticated specimen, perhaps; always a mistake to let them get that way." He paused to take breath amid these unusually extended remarks. "But loyal—one of ourselves as far as this show goes. Killed! By Jove, sir, we'll have their scalps." And Glover looked aggressively round the glade, a sheep belligerent and declared.

"We must remember," said Hoppo, "that we are unarmed. It would be rash—"

"There is no sign of savages—or of any enemy." Appleby sat down on the tree-trunk. "We have no reason to believe that, apart from ourselves, there is a soul within hundreds of miles. So we must do a little thinking. And go carefully with each other. The facts are these." And he gave a brief account of what they had found.

Hoppo, a sheep *à pure et à plein,* looked scared. Glover went immobile, like an organism with limited reactions in the presence of the unknown. And Diana Kittery played with a lizard, as a schoolchild might do who has no need to attend to a lesson a second time.

"And so," said Appleby, "I repeat that we must go carefully. If one of us in this little community turns out to have killed Unumunu what are we going to do? What is it in our power to do? And, to begin with, what attitude is expedient and discreet? I think myself that the mystery is one which we must try to solve. But then I have a professional angle on mysteries and I may be prejudiced."

"We must have the truth if we can." Glover spoke gruffly and with difficulty. "Without it, the situation is intolerable. And then we must decide."

"I agree." Hoppo had braced himself and spoke with unexpected decision. "And it may be that there was great provocation—that there was justification even. We know very little of this oddly westernized Negro whom chance made our companion. And we know little of what relations may . . . there are certain dangers so—" He floundered, picked up a gaping oyster and tried to press it shut; the action seemed to translate itself into some injunction in his mind. "Really," he said, "it is difficult to know just what to say."

"Where," said Diana, "is Miss Curricle?"

7

THE BURIAL OF THE BLACK MAN WAS PUSHED THROUGH against material and spiritual difficulties. Without tools it is not easy to dig a large hole even in sand; without more guidance than an Ethiopian complexion, an Eton accent and a professed interest in anthropology it is hard to determine the extent and character of observances proper to the occasion. Appleby however contrived a grave and Hoppo gave Unumunu what he called the benefit of the doubt. It was finished and they looked uncertainly at the hump of sand that witnessed to it, momentarily aware that this death was in essence no more mysterious than that of the meanest of the ephemeridae in its season. Then, turning to perplexities compassable by the intellect, they wondered again about the absence of Miss Curricle.

It was not yet anything definitively out of the way, not yet adequate ground for the open voicing of suspicion. Anxiety however was reasonable and Glover talked of a search. But even this was premature; Miss Curricle had developed of late a habit that was increasingly solitary. She had, indeed, pronounced against personal relations as likely to be insupportable in the circumstances in which they were placed. There was to be—when her companions' understanding had sufficiently advanced to march with her own—a dark and subliminal communion out of which a strong and primitive new life was to grow. Meanwhile something of the seclusion of the anchorite would help the new consciousness to flower, and between meals —or even over one—Miss Curricle was accustomed to withdraw herself from society. Her ideas, Appleby judged, were not literary in inspiration—from the speculations of dear Lord Tennyson they could scarcely be derived—and their period of incubation was probably painful. Indeed Miss Curricle, wandering the island and discovering herself as an original thinker and fount of the new humanity, was quite likely to go mad. Perhaps this had already happened and the death of Unumunu was a result.

They had soft drinks compounded by Diana and there was an awkward halt which could have been adequately filled only by the reading of a will.

"I think," said Appleby, "that a search ought to be made. We have to hope—unlikely as it seems—that Unumunu's death is evidence of danger from without. So we ought to stick together and find her. And if the danger is domestic—well, the same thing applies. But as a search will miss her as likely as not, I will remain at the base. Perhaps you should all go east—she has been wandering that way—keeping together and getting back before sundown."

Diana finished an enormous drink. "She may be dangerous," she said.

"Any of us may be that." Appleby bestirred himself, hoping for a move. A sudden desire of solitude was upon him—an instinct too that the less said at the moment the better.

But Diana was obstinate. "We should find out who saw him last. And what we have all been doing since. That sort of thing. It's always done." She looked regretfully into her empty gourd. "I thought I saw him just a bit before he—he turned up. But quite likely I was wrong."

"We were all together at breakfast," said Glover. "And then Miss Curricle went off by herself. And then—"

"And then," Hoppo interrupted, "Unumunu went off. He said he was going to make another attempt on the east range. And that left the four of us as we now are." Suddenly he looked extremely acute. "And then until you came back with the news Glover and I were together all the time."

"John and I were together too." Diana nodded sagely. "Practically hand in hand. Practically—" She stopped as if searching for some even more emphatic statement. "Well, practically like that."

Glover coughed. "Hoppo, you are right." He frowned. "No, I don't know that you are. Surely when you were dredging for the oysters and decided to try the farther pool—"

"My dear Glover, you must recall that it proved empty and that not more than five minutes—"

Appleby held up a hasty hand. "I don't think it will be useful to work along these lines at present. Although we were in a sense—er—paired—"

"John"—Diana looked suddenly accusing—"you *did* leave me once—for nearly five minutes, it must have been. Why—"

More urgently this time, Glover coughed. "Really, I agree with Appleby. In the course of a whole day it is natural"—he coughed ferociously—"*strictly* natural, that—"

"We had better be off." Hoppo shaded his eyes and gazed determinedly into distance. "I must confess that I shall be happier in my mind if we find Miss Curricle before dark."

They set out, Diana reluctantly, and Glover and Hoppo somewhat self-consciously armed with cudgels. Appleby watched them depart and then turned to what, in this out-of-the-way hole, must now be called the scene of the crime.

Where had the black man been killed? It would be best to begin with the spot where his body was found, consider the possibilities there, and then move progressively further afield.

The body had been found on a submerged rock surrounded by water. And the water was surrounded on one side by a broad sickle of sand and on the other by a reef sometimes exposed by the tide and sometimes covered to the depth of about a foot. The body had been found with the head smashed in from behind with what might have been either a boulder or some smooth and heavy fabricated weapon.

This was the setting. Suppose, then, Unumunu and another bathing as he and Diana bathed that morning. And suppose them to have reached the submerged rock and the thing to have happened there. It was impossible; the weapon could scarcely have been conveyed there, and certainly not conveyed with concealment; moreover the necessary purchase for a crushing blow could not have been obtained in water or on a fragmentary foothold of rock awash with the sea. Short of such an unknown factor as a boat the crime had no feasibility here.

But in two places in the bay there emerged rocks more considerable than this; on both of them Diana and he had found space to bask in the sun. On one of these the deed might have been done, but again there were difficulties. Boulders or loose rock there were none, so that a weapon would have to be hidden beforehand. And for a premeditated deed of violence such a site was inconveniently open to observation by such tiny population as the island had.

So next came the beach. Appleby tried to imagine himself killing Unumunu there. It would mean walking with him or towards him in an attitude or with a burden which was almost certain to attract attention; it meant then stepping behind him to strike. There was the possibility of approach entirely from behind and unbeknown. But

this would not be easy; with a black man who had not
some scores of generations of tolerable physical security
in his make-up it would probably not be possible at all.
And again the site was public.

And now the jungle—or whatever it was properly to be
called. Here in the half-light of the tree-ferns and amid a
maze of thicket and creeper was the likely place—secrecy,
concealment and the cover of a multitude of small alien
sounds. . . . Appleby, standing yet in the beating sun-
light, stared dubiously into this abrupt cavern of vegetation. He moved towards it up a hillock of loose sand;
slithered and fell. The sand was fine and hot, and there
was a kind of drifting skin to it stirred by an imperceptible
breeze. It was toilsome stuff. And over it and out of the
secrecy of the jungle, over it and across a further stretch of
wet sand, public and taking the lightest imprint of a foot,
the body of Unumunu had presumably been dragged—
dragged for the purpose of pitching it into what was virtually a small sealed lagoon.

Appleby sat down in the shade and longed for tobacco;
perhaps, it occurred to him, one might find it growing
wild on the island if one looked. One might find much
on the island; after all, there was still a stretch of it un-
explored. . . . He returned to the problem of that drag-
ging of a dead and unusually heavy body out of the jungle
and into the bay—in daylight, as it must have been.
Unumunu had wandered off after breakfast; a couple of
hours later Appleby and Diana had been here with the

whole beach under their eye. So here at least were certain limits in point of time.

And time was a factor now, for the tide was coming up. He rose and walked the moist sand from end to end, confirming an impression he had already received; the sand took a clear print which held for minutes only, being rapidly obliterated from below. He tried again higher on the beach, and here he came presently upon traces of movement not accountable by anything known to have happened that day. They told him little except that they had been deliberately confused; he followed them laboriously up the soft sand to the jungle. Just here Unumunu's body had been lugged out on the beach . . . he moved into the shadows and sat down to let his eyes accommodate themselves to the shade.

For a moment the air about him was alive with the whirr of tiny wings; then it fell stagnant again—hot, moist and of the earth. The crickets outvoiced the distant fall of breakers beyond the farther reef; the clumsy stealth of lizards was about his feet; before his nose the fleshy mouth of a monstrous scarlet flower closed suddenly on a fly. Never, he thought, could mortal have essayed criminal investigation in an atmosphere more blatantly assertive of the irrelevance of human justice, of the fictitiousness of the conception that nature moves because before it there beckon desirable goals. Here evidently things moved only because there was always a shove from behind; things happened exclusively because other things had happened before. And Unumunu's murder interested him—as all his other murders and allied horrors had done —simply because it was a species of occurrence in which the identity of the shoves from behind was particularly teasing. Particularly teasing and therefore, in the solution, particularly capable of gratifying that appetite for power, for assertive shoving on from behind, which seems to be the only dynamic principle nature will reveal. . . .

Appleby, who was not a philosopher, straightened his back in sudden reproach and dismay. It was probably over a hundred in the shade, and these speculative inclinations must be put down to that. He turned his inner eye to the contemplation of his companions and found them papery and thin, as if they obstinately preserved the phantasmic nature of their final days on the waters. Hoppo, indeed, had been more real when implicated with the Seven Sacred Cataracts; Glover more considerable when much was to be suffered and little to be done. As for Diana, although it would be extremely irrational in him to deny her the most emphatic physical existence, she had the character of evaporating from the mind when any picture of the dead man and his fate rose in it. Miss Curricle alone remained for anything resembling agreeable professional speculation. And Appleby suspected that Miss Curricle, in theory so deviously determined to lie with men, was in fact of those who incurably walk with the gods—with Proteus or the great Poseidon in the Tonga Trench, with Lilith the mother of all living in a fable that has long grown dim.

She was not a woman with more than a veneer of the practical mind. She would murder an antipathetic notion, supposing notions to be susceptible of summary elimination in that way. She might murder a man if he stood for or embodied a notion. But it was difficult to see how Unumunu could have done that.

Appleby shook his head—and found a little crowd of flies rise in air. This was not the way to solve a mystery. It was not thus that he had plumbed the matter of Dr. Umpleby and the bones, of the stylish homicides at Scamnum Court, of the daft laird of Erchany; it was not thus that he had exposed the Friends of the Venerable Bede or preserved ten persons from the blackest suspicion by recollecting a line in *The Ancient Mariner*. It was not thus— He stood up with a groan. A cursed climate. He should not so be floored, even by the devious exertions of an odd day. He was a prematurely aged young man, aimlessly reminiscing.

Unumunu had been hauled on and across the beach here. The disturbance in the fringe of jungle was visible; there was a distinguishable trail in the undergrowth, as one might expect when a heavy body had recently been dragged through. He followed the trail for perhaps twenty yards, only to find himself cheated. With the tropical unaccountability which marked it in more ways than one, the jungle changed character; everywhere was a rubbery and resilient growth that had taken no impression from whatever had passed. He cast about for some

time and in vain; he could find no further trail. So he reflected on what he had found—reflected until its unreason
stared out at him. For the trail as he had traced it ran
parallel to the beach, and so continued, likely enough,
where it was invisible. Very laboriously the black man's
body had been lugged through the shelter of the jungle's
fringe to the point at which cover had been broken in a
scramble to the beach. But throughout that twenty yards
or more of stumbling progress the beach and the bay had
lain equally accessible and near. . . . Appleby foraged an
armful of sticks and went down once more to the water.

Sticks, thrown far into the bay, came sluggishly but
invariably back. As the tide was coming in this was
scarcely surprising. But Appleby, seeming to ignore the
labour-saving principle of induction, walked slowly along
the beach throwing in more sticks. As he came near the
point at which the body had been dragged down, their
behaviour became uncertain; when he was abreast of
the point it changed. The sticks now floated away and
disappeared.

Impelled by some inner excitement, he turned and
doubled up the beach; he found a hollow log and into each
end jammed a stone; he collected more sticks. He returned to the water's edge and pitched in the log. Almost
awash, it floated away; he doubled back once more to
higher ground from which it could be observed. The
nearer reef, all above water still, appeared to stretch con-
tinuously across the bay. But on reaching the barrier the

-⟨ 69 ⟩-

log momentarily disappeared from sight, to become visible again in the further bay. Somewhere there was a channel and, ebb or flow, a current ran out through it to the ocean.

And now Appleby threw stick after stick from the same point, and stick after stick disappeared. It was a strong and certain current, stronger even than those which he and Diana had tackled that morning. . . . He continued to throw sticks. And the fortieth stick defied prediction, glided on an aberrant course, ended by eddying round the now wholly submerged rock where Unumunu's body had been found.

Appleby threw away his remaining sticks and turned a sober face towards what, conventionally, might be called home. The island's short twilight was drawing on.

8

THE GLADE—CAUTIOUSLY APPROACHED—PROVED UNTEN-
anted; the search-party had not yet returned. That it ever
would return was now a purely speculative proposition,
and Appleby was inclined to regret that he had encouraged it to set out. But probably you were as safe on one
corner of the island as another—perhaps safer on the
move than waiting amid a gathering darkness at a base.

The crickets had fallen silent. From the reef the breakers murmured their message of isolation and of the world
forgot and, inland, an unknown creature screamed in
short, decisive agony. There was now a star, terribly remote, in the irregular patch of darkening sky above;
underfoot, the jacaranda carpet glowed momentarily
vivid before being taken by the night. . . . Appleby
paused on the edge of the glade and summarized the position as best he could.

He was on an island. For this he had the evidence of
his eyes, laboriously transported to a central eminence
the day before. From this point, perhaps two thousand
feet up and inevitably named Mount Ararat, there could
be seen a girdle of unbroken ocean. That the island formed
part of a group there was no sign, nor was there any sign

of an objective correlative to the mirage which, at sea-level, sometimes appeared at sunset. The island stood alone, and a fair amount of wandering had disposed them to believe that they stood alone on the island. Its total extent was not great, and only one area—screened both from sight and ready access by a spur running east from Mount Ararat—was unknown to them; it could be little more, this, than a strip of coast.

Appleby shivered—not because of the sinister possibilities on the fringe of his mind, but simply because at sundown it grew suddenly cold. Commonly they lit a great fire. He stepped into the glade and persuaded himself that he was concentrating his mind on whether one should be lit tonight. He was conscious of moving as in a shallow well of faint and diffused light around which were dark walls of jungle. He passed the little palisade of brush and palm-leaves that was Diana's sleeping-quarters, passed a similar structure of Miss Curricle's—and stopped. Before him now was a contrivance of Glover's in course of construction, a sort of wash-place composed of stones and clay. It was not entirely a success, for in places the clay remained obstinately damp. And at one of these places he was looking now, his eye held by something just evident in the failing light. What he saw was a single footprint in the damp clay—the single print of five toes and the ball of a foot. He stared at it, patently astounded and obscurely disturbed. Man Friday had appeared, and in a great hurry at that. He knelt down with sudden

minute interest in the thing; rose with an air of something like conviction. He stood still, trying to weigh
chances as they might be interpreted on the evidence of
half-forgotten books. Then he went over to the fire-place
and knelt down once more, vulnerable as in a dream, and
blew on the embers. There was kindling-wood to hand
and within a few minutes the fire flared as usual. He fell to
preparing what Glover called dinner and Diana tea. It
occurred to him to whistle and he whistled an approxi-
mation to the overture of *Figaro*, stuff strictly musical
but related nevertheless to the common emotion of joy.
And now night had really fallen.

There was Diana's pigeon of the morning—Diana's and
the black man's pigeon—to bake in a shell of clay. The
black man had been *black;* perhaps there was something in
that. Moreover he had possessed certain specific curiosi-
ties; perhaps there was something in that too. Appleby
stiffened at a sound from the darkness. He relaxed; it was
a clumsy sound. He smiled into the fire as there became
audible the tired and pettishly apologizing voice of Hoppo.

"Really, Glover, I had no idea you were in front.
Appleby has the fire going, I am glad to see. It is useless
to deny that one result of our anxieties is something uncommonly like an appetite. I believe there is a pigeon
baking. How terrible it all is! Like a dream of dreams. I
wish we possessed some tea. Nothing is more refreshing.
Mrs. Kittery, I thought you were a tree. Dreadful! Dreadful, indeed." And Hoppo, mildly distracted, came un-

certainly into the firelight.

"You have bad news?" Appleby poked briskly at the embers.

"We have not found Miss Curricle. But we have found —it is most disturbing—we have found"—Hoppo, now close to the fire, glanced from Glover to Diana as if for aid—"we have found her garments."

"What?"

"Means her clothes." Glover spoke huskily and abruptly. "Half way up the east range we found her clothes in a heap. Disagreeable—whichever way one looks at it, you know. *All* her clothes." He cleared his throat awkwardly. "Or at least so Mrs. Kittery thinks probable."

"It is to be hoped," said Hoppo, "that it is an aberation merely." He sat down and looked about him for food. "Speaking confidentially—or rather speaking *openly*, for that is the better phrase—I have some ground for supposing—that is to say I am inclined to think—that Miss Curricle's mind has—um—been running increasingly in certain channels, *regrettable* channels—"

"Gone off her head, in fact." Glover interrupted abruptly. "No need to make a mouthful of it. Poor lady gone through great hardships. And these things happen. Mrs. Kittery here—woman of the world—face facts—" And Glover became inarticulate in his turn.

Diana was unfolding a small bundle. "Here's her slip. And here—"

Hastily Appleby gave her a long drink. "I understand what you mean. Miss Curricle has her own ideas on how one must come to live if thrown on a desert island. And a certain measure of nudism might be one of the particulars." He paused. "Has any of you thought of another explanation?"

"Of course we have. And seen something like evidence, too." Glover picked up a yam and held it suspended while he finished what he had to say. "We went on and got to the top of the range. And down in a farther valley we saw a column of smoke. It looked as if it might come from a fairly big fire."

"The sort of fire," said Diana, "on which one could— could imagine an *enormous* pot." She took up a stone and neatly uncased the pigeon. "A pot—to face facts, as the Colonel says—with Miss Curricle inside." For a moment Diana looked quite sad. "And, John—has anything happened to you?"

For answer he drew a brand from the fire and led them over to the wash-place. For a moment they stared at the footprint in silence. "Mrs. Kittery," Glover asked doubtfully, "might it be yours?"

Diana shook her head. Appleby spoke. "The relation of the big toe to the others is not that of a foot that has been habitually confined in a shoe. Look how naturally it has come down with a gap between—much as a European *hand* might come down. And I have another piece of news. Unumunu was killed by a person or persons with a remarkable knowledge of the island and the currents about it." He recounted his experiments. "You see, the body was so disposed of that the chances were about forty to one in favour of its drifting straight out to the ocean. Unumunu would just have disappeared and we should never have known how."

"Savages!" said Hoppo. "Oh dear, oh dear!"

"Much better than the suspicion that the devilry was our own affair," said Glover.

"And," said Diana, "it gives Mr. Hoppo scope. I can think of another book. *Mr. Hoppo's Heathen.* John, they will be heathen, won't they?"

"Assuredly." Appleby led the way back to the fire. "Did anything further happen on the range?"

Glover shook his head. "It was too late to go on, even if we had not had Mrs. Kittery to consider. We should have been caught by darkness on impossible ground. But tomorrow—"

"*A common fate.*" Diana, staring wide-eyed into the fire, pronounced the words with great emphasis. "I'm sorry to interrupt. But it's just occurred to me. A common fate. That's what you say when the same thing happens to people—isn't it?"

They assured her that it was.

"Well, what I mean is that the same thing *hasn't* happened to Ponto and Miss Curricle. And it's odd, I think. I mean, if Miss Curricle is for the pot why go to ever such a sweat to float poor Ponto out to the sharks? There's a—a—"

"Discrepancy," offered Appleby. He too was staring at the fire, but with narrowed lids. And his voice was that of an abstracted man as he went on. "But there is very little reason to suppose that Miss Curricle has been put in a pot. Even if she has fallen into the hands of savages they need not be cannibals. Perhaps they have floated her out to sea too. Or, again, it is possible that they might not harm her. Unumunu was a black man and perhaps more likely to be taken as an enemy and less likely to be received as a wonder. He was also an anthropologist and, having discovered natives, may have poked indiscreetly into some particularly private rite. Perhaps he was disposed of so summarily because of something like that. As for Miss Curricle, for all we know they may now be worshipping her as a goddess. It is to be hoped that a robe or two has been supplied." He continued, unsmiling, to stare into the fire. "I believe I should have done better," he added enigmatically, "if my education had consisted in taking out classes too." He paced up and down, and the movement was not in harmony with the fluent string of possibilities he had been propounding. "And now there is the question of immediate policy. We can't very confidently reckon on all being taken for divinities—"

"Not even Mrs. Kittery." Hoppo beamed at his own sudden and outlandish gallantry; then his glance went to the jungle and the beam faded. "It may have been imagination," he said, "but I thought I discerned—" He stopped. From somewhere startlingly close at hand there came the dull slow pulse of a drum.

Glover reached for his cudgel; the others stayed very still. The sound was an abrupt declaration of danger, short-circuiting speculation, removing doubt. But it was also something inside. Each beat was like a potent capsule of fear dissolving in the blood, and if the poisoned stream reached the heart perhaps the heart would stop. . . . And now, from across the glade, there came the pulse of an answering drum, faster, like some rapid beast of prey coming down a long tunnel and edging past a lumbering mate. There was a moment of confusion in the tunnel— the tunnel that was deep inside the listening self—and then the rhythms joined and the creatures became one; there was one rushing monster intent to drive them far down the tunnel, to drive them down a tunnel which would sink them aeons deep in a primitive past. One had to grab at the sides—and Appleby grabbed. It was true, then, what was said about the power of drums . . . in *The Plumed Serpent*, for instance. And based on such overpowering experiences as this were the attenuated thrills of poetry and the dance. Appleby, grabbing thus at the civilized consciousness, was enabled to speak in the most briskly unemotional way.

"Colonel, I don't think we'll prepare for a fight. It's almost certain that the odds would be hopeless. We must beat our own drums."

Glover put down the cudgel. "What d'you mean?"

"The drums are magic being brought against us. Remember how strange we may be. Nothing but the bare report of white men may ever have reached these people before. We must keep our own magic going and not let it be disturbed by theirs. Diana, would you please pass the salt?" Appleby sat down again at the table they had improvised for meals. "Hoppo, may I help you to half a pigeon?"

Hoppo, who had been peering apprehensively into the darkness, turned round. To be let in on the pigeon was more than he had hoped.

"Please. And I believe you are right. A display of *le sang froid*." He giggled uncertainly. "To keep us from joining Miss Curricle in *l'eau chaud*."

As ceremoniously as the gleanings of a sun-deck café would permit, they continued to dine. The drums, though again nearer, were not so terrifying after all; sophisticate the rhythm ever so slightly and there would result something very like the music to which thousands of civilized persons willingly dined every night. Even the howls—for it was undeniable that now the savages were intermittently howling as well—were not unlike those which the members of a well-trained band will sporadically emit. The experiment of carrying on undisturbed, tentatively and dubiously begun, was well under way.

"Perhaps," said Diana, "it hasn't really anything to do

with us. Perhaps they're just making corroborree on their own. Perhaps, even, later"—she turned serious eyes from one to another of her companions—"we might be able to stroll across and have a look."

Glover shook his head decisively. "Certainly not. That sort of thing . . . most unsuitable. Thoroughly indecent, as often as not. Why, even in India—"

He stopped—stopped because the drums had suddenly fallen silent. The jungle was very still; on its nearer walls their camp-fire stirred uncertain shadows; in the undergrowth it was possible to imagine one saw the gleam of eyes. And then something like a shooting star flashed across the vault above. As they looked another passed, and then another and another. Just above their heads was a criss-cross of fire. This vanished and there was a moment of darkness; then a single dart of light shot high in air and fell. In the centre of the table before them stood a flaming spear.

They stared as if their vision had been transfixed by the barbaric still-quivering thing. Glover reached for his cudgel once more. And as he did so there came a crash from the darkness and into the firelight leapt a naked and coppery body, brandishing a fellow to the weapon in front of them. Another leap and he was in silhouette and gigantic against the fire; beside him a second figure had risen as if from earth; from the darkness beyond rose a single concerted howl.

It was a moment, thought Appleby, to push a counter-magic to an extreme. He rose and held up his gourd.

"Mrs. Kittery and gentlemen," he said, "the King!"

They stood up as if drilled. The toast was honoured. And now it was the monstrous creatures before them who appeared transfixed, staring at the incomprehensible ritual. For seconds the thing held like a tableau. Then the naked figures yelled, turned, fled. And in the darkness beyond their cowardice precipitated a rout. A yelling and crashing in sharp diminuendo filled the air. Silence followed, in which the diners could hear each other gasp. Only the spear which still smouldered on the table was evidence that the incident had not been dreamed.

Appleby leant forward and grabbed the weapon, as if only its substantial reality in his hand would suffice. The shaft was of bamboo, the head appeared to be of bone, near it was a charred remnant of some stuff like tow. It was hard to believe in the possibility of meeting such a thing outside a museum. Appleby fingered it, poised it, even sniffed at it like a dog. Then he handed it to Glover.

"Booty," he said; "the foundations of our armoury. Your department, sir."

Glover took his eyes from the jungle to examine the spear. He grunted, his professional interest caught.

"Dashed ugly thing. Easy to in with and nasty to get out. I remember on the North-West Frontier—"

Appleby was not attending. But neither did his senses appear to be directed to the still dangerous world without; he was looking at Diana as absently as an overworked

-< 81 >-

tourist confronted with yet another goddess in the Louvre. Glover's reminiscence remained unuttered, and it was Hoppo who next spoke.

"A tree," he suggested. "I wonder if we could get up a tree?"

Dubiously balancing the spear, Glover snorted. "Tree? To be reduced to the condition of savages ourselves is about enough, without descending to the damned monkeys. We must stick by the fire until morning and then march out on these fellows and show we're not afraid of them. You've just seen that line work. No shame in being treed by a tiger, sir—but by savages not."

"I really don't think my suggestion unreasonable." Hoppo was obstinate. "Somebody was talking of *The Swiss Family Robinson* and, you know, they lived in a tree because of savages. And as for monkeys—"

"*Hoppo's Hop.*" Diana, having discovered this new and brilliant variant on her favourite joke, let her laughter ring through the night.

"Really, Mrs. Kittery, you are easily diverted. And the Swiss Family Robinson were very sensible people—"

"Sir," broke in Glover with vehemence and finality, "the Swiss Family Robinson were *Swiss.*"

"They hadn't a king to toast," said Diana. "The Swiss are only a—a—"

"Republican federation on the cantonal system," supplied Appleby. "Will you all be quiet?"

They listened. And again something was happening in the jungle; there was a stealthy, almost irresolute movement on the edge of the glade. It ceased and a voice called out—the voice of Miss Curricle.

"Mrs. Kittery," it called, "Mrs. Kittery, will you please come here?" It rose a pitch. "And *only* Mrs. Kittery, please; I insist on that."

It was like a voice from the past—or from the pot. Hoppo appeared even to think of ghosts, for he stood up in agitation. "It may be—" he broke off. "It may be a trap."

"Stuff and nonsense." Glover jumped up too. "Miss Curricle—"

"Go away, sir." Miss Curricle's voice, though issuing from an impenetrable darkness, rose in further sharp agitation. "I have met with a most embarrassing misadventure. Mrs. Kittery, please, I must insist."

Diana was rummaging by the firelight. "Miss Curricle," she called out wickedly, "is it your clothes you want? We have them here."

"You have them!" The voice was extremely indignant.

"Only I can't lay my hands on them. I think, perhaps, that Mr. Hoppo—"

"Mr. Hoppo, how dare you perpetrate such an impertinence?" In the blackness branches crackled beneath Miss Curricle's indignation.

"Dear lady"—Hoppo's voice rose in its turn in horrid distress—"I assure you that no offensive jest was designed. The garments appeared abandoned . . . we are only too relieved . . . it was much to be feared—"

Diana had slipped away with the clothes; Glover had retreated tactfully in an opposite direction; Appleby sat wrapped in his own thoughts and waited for this deplorable comedy to play itself out. And presently Miss Curricle, clothed and aggressively in her right mind, was sitting by the fire and eating the remains of dinner.

"We are dreadfully sorry," Diana said. "But we *did* find the clothes and they *did* seem to be abandoned. We thought you mightn't need them any more; we thought that—well, that you were beyond clothes."

"Beyond clothes!" Miss Curricle's tones hinted embarrassment as well as indignation.

"We thought you had been eaten."

"Eaten? You must have taken leave of your senses. But it is true that"—she hesitated—"that I did abandon my clothes. In our circumstances, in our circumstances as I then envisaged them—" she broke off. "But I need not enter into that. My resolution has proved to be premature."

Appleby studied Miss Curricle in the uncertain light and thought that, indefinably, she had gone angular again —that this, in fact, was once more the Miss Curricle who had presided over the sun-deck café before Mr. Hoppo had erroneously announced the appearance of a whale. Not, perhaps, wholly this anterior Miss Curricle, for the lady before him had the air of casting—figuratively—one longing lingering look behind. But as near as made no difference. "Premature?" he prompted gently.

"Exactly. I have discovered that our circumstances are not to be so—so near to nature as I had supposed. The island is inhabited."

"There!" said Diana. "And that's why we thought you were a goner. You see, they killed poor Ponto this morning."

"Killed Sir Ponto!" Miss Curricle looked alarmed, but obviously not for the reason they might have supposed. She glanced from one to another. "I begin to fear that the privations to which you have been exposed—"

"Will you tell us"—again Appleby interrupted gently —"just what has been happening to you?"

"I succeeded in climbing the eastern range and making my way along the crest. And then below, on the edge of a fairly large bay, I saw a building."

"Ah!" exclaimed Glover, "the club-house."

"The club-house? No, I didn't see that."

"Did you," asked Diana, "see any canoes?"

"Or bodies," said Hoppo, suddenly ghoulish, "—desiccated bodies on poles?" He looked wistfully at the tree-tops faintly silhouetted against the night.

"Certainly not. I tell you I saw a building. A *real* building. And it said something on the roof."

"On the roof?" Hoppo giggled feebly. "Said something?"

Miss Curricle nodded, angular and defeated. "In big white letters. *Hotel*."

9

Dawn on the island came like a blind going up on a prospect of hot-houses, like a cover being removed from a crowded bird-cage, like a lid lifted from a crate of monkeys. At one moment the palms slumbered, propped against the stars; the jungle was lonely, dark and void; only the ocean sounded, murmuring ceaselessly into the ear of night. And the next moment there was rustle and chatter and the stealing of sunbeams everywhere; curled and crumpled green-coverletted flowers unfolded their blue and scarlet with the measured speed of a man turning over and stretching himself in bed; lizards lumbered out of holes and exercised their darting tongues; parrots squandered a pandemonium of cries amid the tunnels and colonnades of fern. From the recesses of the place there came a brief stirring of innumerable scents, as if some subtly aromatic creature had begun to breathe again, and through the moss of tiny rides and brief green bottoms runnels and freshets trickled as if at the turning of a master tap. The total sensation was of something primeval and pristine at once. Down the tall trees the light ran as if in a first embrace. And up to the sky one could raise one's arms like Adam and cry *Morning!* to a novel world.

Colonel Glover, sentinel by the dying fire, contrived something not unlike this. "Dashed fine," he said. "Bright and early's the best time in most parts of the world. And bright and early's the tip for us today. Civilization's round the corner unless that woman's clean crazed. And with luck we'll make it by noon."

Appleby, who had been prowling in search of such tracks as savages in flight might be supposed to leave, fell to preparing breakfast on the embers.

"I don't think she's crazed. The process is rather the other way. I believe in that hotel. A slender draught of tropic isle intoxicated the brain. And now, when we reach the pub, drinking largely will sober us again." He laughed —partly because the joke gained excellence from the morning, partly because Glover looked bewildered and unamused. "But it doesn't alter the fact of what happened last night, nor yet yesterday morning. I'm sorry they got that black man before we contacted the world. He interested me."

"Unumunu was a bit of a queer fish, if you ask my opinion." Glover shook his head doubtfully. "All the instincts of a gentleman, as far as one could see. And his father can have been no more than a savage beating his tom-tom in the jungle. Not natural, sir. And—talking of tom-toms—we haven't contacted the world yet. Lord knows what ambush may be waiting for us. Hard on these women." He coughed. "Fine creatures, Appleby; stood up to a lot. That Mrs. Kittery—a bit of a filly, of course, as you know." He coughed again. "As you may guess, I mean. But a courageous woman. And comes from some God-awful hole in the Bush, as like as not. Makes one proud of the Empire." Glover, thus unveiling his soul under the influence of dawn, concealed embarrassment by scowling ferociously at the jungle. "And Miss Curricle too . . . awkward moments, of course—but difficult age, you know . . . gallant creature." He rose abruptly. "Baked eggs? Delicious. Better be rousing them up. Never quite know the civil way to do it, though. Can't knock at the door."

"Wake Hoppo and send him."

"Good. He'll tell them to get on their garments." Glover gave a rare chuckle. "Good fellow, though, Hoppo. Sound views, unless thrown off his balance. We've been lucky, when you come to think of it. Might have been landed with some awful bounders, just pitched into the sea like that." He paused in his stride, a new thought striking him. "Foreigners, even." He marched off.

Appleby continued to get breakfast, knitting his brows over it more than the simple operations involved required. The black of Unumunu and the copper of last night's savage visitors made sombre compositions in his head. Unumunu they were leaving behind—leaving behind, if Miss Curricle's story was true, in another world. Exchange the desert-island presumption for even the slenderest outpost of civilization, and the outlandish Sir Ponto and his fate would tumble into the past. Appleby, for whom no homicide was complete without a sequel in the criminal court, felt that it was necessary to adjust his habits of mind to local conditions. Raiding savages were presumably accountable to somebody for deeds of violence, but a bird of passage from Scotland Yard was scarcely involved. . . . He set out the breakfast and walked rapidly into the jungle.

There was that hovering suggestion of land at sunset. He reached the edge of the lagoon and stared out to sea. Westward, visibility would never be better than at this hour, but to all his scanning the horizon presented an unbroken line of blue once more. And it had done this from the summit of Ararat, though then atmospheric conditions had been less satisfactory. He turned back to the loose, dry sand, already hot from the sun, and to the jungle-fringe beyond. He plunged into the undergrowth and, in imagination, took the weight of Unumunu's dead body in his arms. And then he looked at the beach below. The riddle of the sands.

The riddle of the sands, he repeated to himself—and suddenly shaded his eyes to stare intently into distance. For at the farthest tip of the long sickle of beach below him there had appeared something like an enormous turtle. But a gaily hued turtle, rather like a vast version of a tortoise in an Oxford quadrangle, or Maryland's terrapin, sportively painted with the colours of its college. The creature showed quarterings of red and green, and it moved forward, invisibly propelled, by the edge of the

sea. For a moment Appleby thought of the savages pro-
ducing some new device of surprise. And then he saw
that he was looking at an umbrella—at an umbrella something between the outsized employed by golfers and the
yet larger variety commonly met with at seaside resorts.
Beneath this there was presently visible a pair of white-
flannelled legs. Trotting by the legs was a Sealyham dog.
And the whole advanced through the emptiness of the
morning with a mild purposiveness and an even pace.

Appleby again thought of the Swiss Family. In that
immortal book the good pastor showed no surprise when
his sons brought him word now of lions and penguins,
now of tigers and polar bears. Here too one would
quickly lose the sense of the incongruous: hotels and
savages in the jungle, black corpses and white flannels on
the beach. But unique among all these was the fact that
the approaching figure could be interrogated. Appleby
scrambled down and hurried forward.

The flannelled legs halted. The Sealyham halted too.
And a voice from beneath the umbrella called out: "Don't
be alarmed. George is a very quiet dog."

Appleby, to whom it had not occurred that George
might be among the hazards of island life, continued his
progress. And now the umbrella tilted and revealed a
comfortable figure, dark glasses and an immaculate
panama hat. The hat came off and the voice said courteously: "How do you do?" The phrase, instead of being
given the faintly threatening inflection which standard

English requires, was uttered as a genuine query, so that Appleby found himself obliged to reply that he was very well. The stranger smiled, as if really pleased. And George wagged his tail.

There was a pause and Appleby thought he might try a question of his own. "Are you from the hotel?"

George growled. The stranger's brow discernibly clouded. "No," he said, "I am not—I ought to say *we* are not"—and he stooped to pat George—"in any way connected with the hotel. Except in the merest and most occasional social duty. . . . I ought to say my name is Hailstone—Gregory Hailstone." He paused, obscurely expectant. "I suppose," he added wistfully, "you don't happen to be a digging man?"

Appleby, without precisely understanding what was implied, thought it safe to reply that he was not. There had, of course, been the troublesome business of burying Unumunu, but the stranger could scarcely be referring to that sort of thing.

"My name is John Appleby," he said. "I am a police officer from London."

"Ah. One does occasionally long so for professional contacts. And, of course, it is possible that we have a common interest in bones." Hailstone smiled. His smile seemed achieved with effort, so that Appleby wondered if the muscles involved were habitually unexercised. "Though not, perhaps of the same vintage." And Hailstone smiled again, but patently with more effort than before. Appleby looked at George, who had sunk very gently down on his stomach. The point about a smile, he saw, was that a certain quantum of physical impulsion was required. And on the island one learnt to be economical in such expenditures.

"If you are unconnected with the hotel," said Appleby, "perhaps you have something to do with the savages?"

George lifted his black nose just sufficiently to give his lower jaw room to drop. He yawned. And Hailstone looked as if he might almost yawn too.

"Dear me, no. The natives are uninteresting—quite uninteresting. They have been quite devoid of interest for several centuries. I would positively prefer the folk in the hotel."

"The natives are of some interest to me. One of my companions has been murdered by them." Appleby pointed over Hailstone's shoulder. "And, talking of bones, that's his grave."

This time it was Hailstone who took the initiative; he gave a little jump a split second before George.

"Impossible!" he exclaimed. "If the natives were in the slightest degree dangerous we should have endeavoured to contact you the moment you were heard of. They might offer some sort of demonstration, but they would certainly not commit murder."

"They murdered Sir Ponto Unumunu."

"You are joking. Such an outlandish name can only be a joke."

"He was a Negro—an educated Negro. As for a demonstration, we have certainly had that too."

"A Negro? That might make some difference, I suppose." Hailstone scanned the beach with a sort of placid apprehensiveness. "Yes, it is most unfortunate. It might even give them a taste—" He broke off and turned his blue-spectacled gaze to the lagoon. "The launch has been hunting for you further north. But it should be in here at any time, and I really think we had better collect your companions and be off. Not that there is any danger." He waved limply towards the horizon. "The natives will certainly have made off. But on the other side we are all eager to welcome you—are we not, George?"

George, who had found it supremely restful to let his chin sink down upon his paws, turned upon Appleby an upwards glance which contrived to wring eloquence out of the dumb condition to which he had been born. Then he let his eyelids droop and began to snore.

"You were seen a couple of days ago, but the launch had broken down and nobody would come round. It is difficult to keep people at all on their toes in this part of the world."

George snored loudly.

"And now perhaps you will introduce me to your companions? I can hardly restrain my impatience at the prospect of new faces." Hailstone momentarily removed his glasses and regarded Appleby with amiable but lukewarm attention. His face was yellow and fleshy, untanned by the sun; there was about it some indefiniteness or ambiguity which was hard to place. He lowered his umbrella and tapped George on the rump. They all moved slowly up the beach. "I am doing a dig. Or rather I am going to do a dig; it is difficult, you know, to get people on the move." He stopped again, appearing to find that conversation and pedestrianism could not conveniently be combined. "About your man who has been killed—we must send a message to the Governor."

"There is a Governor on the island?"

"Dear me, no. On another island. I have never been quite sure where. In fact, I rather believe he moves about. He eats up one island and then moves to another. Rather like a sovereign progressing among his nobles in mediaeval times. But he is always on the same wave-length. I am sure he will send a boat for you if you wish. Only unfortunately our wireless has broken down. All technical skills tend to break down here, I have noticed. Even George's tricks are not what they used to be." Hailstone offered these disjointed communications with ample pauses in between. "I suppose you were wrecked?"

"Torpedoed."

"Dear me—how all that spreads! Here on the island it is difficult to realize—"

Appleby moved resolutely forward. "By the way, Mr. Hailstone, what is your island called?"

"Called?" Hailstone stopped again, the energies available to him being apparently diverted into the channels of memory. George stopped too and raised a hind paw to scratch rather perplexedly at an ear. "I'm afraid it hasn't got a name—not yet. I arrived first, so the job of naming it is really mine. And I have deferred the matter, feeling that one day a particularly appealing name will turn up. I have suggested George Island, but unfortunately there were objections from the hotel." Hailstone lowered his voice, as one might do had one a confidential communication to make in a tube lift. "I am afraid I am being disingenuous. The island *has* a name. Viking Island. Only as yet nobody must know."

"Dear me." Appleby found the mild expletive infectious. "May I ask if a similar secrecy marks its whereabouts? I fancy I have seen land miraging up to the west."

"Ah. Some of the islands do behave oddly. I sometimes think they must be like Alcinous's island in the *Odyssey*. Do you read Greek?"

"Yes. I thought I saw land to the west."

"Just another island. Probably the one the natives are on. The group is very scattered. But the first real *land* one would come to towards the west would be Australia. And to the east—and at about the same distance—one would come to the Isthmus of Panama. In fact we may be described as enjoying a central situation." Hailstone laughed—carefully without vehemence, like a patient recovering from an abdominal operation. He turned towards the sea. "Ah, there they are."

The faint chug of a petrol-engine could be heard at a distance, and with it came a waft, a broken phrase, a

sudden wailing continuity of music. Again Appleby had
the sense of incongruities piling up. Faintly in the advancing sound he could hear the beat of drums—drums
not unlike those which had pulsed so powerfully in the
night. But above the drums was a sob and moan of outlandish wood-winds and trumpets. Over the dazzle of the
water, gliding by the coral, cutting across the image of a
palm, there was somewhere advancing all the parapher-
nalia of the dance, locked in the magic sound-track of a
disk. A worn disk, rightly wailing that it wasn't so young
any more, mournfully asserting the thousand miles of its
travels, gallantly announcing its intention of hanging its
hat on the Bam-bam-bammy shore.

And I ain't so young any more. . . .
The music was suddenly vibrant as round the curve of
the further reef shot a long white motor-launch. It held
a little crowd of people in topees, sun-glasses, skimpy
bathers and purposively designed beach suits.

"The hotel, you know," said Hailstone. He spoke with
what was almost haste. "They are combining your rescue
with a little expedition—fishing, and so on. Curious, too,
no doubt. Not in very good taste, perhaps; but there you
are."

The launch turned on the water with a flash of scrubbed
paint and burnished brass, turned again as if keeping time
to the thrumming tune. At the helm an indeterminate but
commanding figure—Appleby had a glimpse, beggaring
description, of flowing skirts and a beard—called an order;

the engine faltered and stopped; the bathers and beach suits uncurled, straightened, bent and coiled again as if deliberately adorning the scene with a slow, plastic voluptuousness; at the prow a business-like sailor appeared with a boat-hook; the music rose and hit the sense with a final blare and cry; in sudden silence the launch and its company glided across the inner lagoon. And in golden letters on the side Appleby could read the words:

Heaven's Hermitage Hotel.

10

"Is everything," asked Appleby, "as out of date as their dance tunes?"

Hailstone shook his head. "The hotel is very insistent that it offers *confort moderne*. But Mrs. Heaven—the woman in the stern there—is something of an artist in her way. She thinks that the establishment should preserve as much of the atmosphere of the later twenties as it can. The thirties give the feeling, I suppose, of being too near the Deluge. . . . George, mind your manners."

George was backing slowly up the beach, as if a sea on which there floated Mrs. Heaven's launch was not one in which he would care to wet his paws. Now he paused, a dog learned and aloof, and viewed the scene with austere distaste, like an ancient satirist contemplating the Ship of Fools. From the launch some one was tactlessly whistling the rapid and monotonous whistle with which common dogs are summoned. George turned round and lay down with his behind presented to the offensive scene.

"Of course," continued Hailstone, "I must stop and introduce you. Not that I know any of those people very well. I believe they are known as the Younger Crush. Now they've got out their little gangway. Yes, the woman in front is Miss Busst, the leader of the Younger Crush."

"The fat woman who seems to have rheumatism?" asked Appleby.

"Yes. And the bald man behind is Mr. Rumsby, the most prominent of the Younger Crush men. They are just handing him his stick. His sister, Mrs. Sadgrove, is not there. She counts as a Younger Matron, I believe—but now seldom leaves her bed. There is Sir Mervyn Poulish; I am told he was at one time prominent in the City but has been in close retirement for years. Indeed, all these people are seekers of retirement, I suppose. But I do rather wish they hadn't sought it on my island. It makes the servant problem difficult for one thing. If only the natives were as violent as you appear to believe we might get them to chase Heaven's whole angelic circle away." And Hailstone gave something between a chuckle and a sigh.

"They appear," said Appleby, watching the party now approaching along the beach, "to be rather old for their roles."

"It's like the people on a cruise—have you noticed?" Hailstone cocked up his blue-spectacled face with sudden scientific incisiveness. "Go for a cruise and you get a glimpse of the western world forty years on. No young people worth speaking of. The birth rate down and the death rate up and the mean age of the population rising every year. It might solve some problems. . . . This war" —Hailstone was vague again—"very disturbing—you must tell me about it sometime. . . . Ah, Mrs. Heaven, how do you do?"

Mrs. Heaven was not in beach clothes; she was the bearded lady in skirts. And her stride had the same embarrassing masculinism as her features; she was ahead of the uncertainly moving Miss Busst and Mr. Rumsby and with a jerked-out nod to Hailstone addressed Appleby direct.

"The ladies," she said; "did they save their jewels?"

"I fear not many. We were torpedoed during the day and while they were on deck."

"Oh." Mrs. Heaven looked glum. "How sad for them. Welcome to the Hermitage. What's your name? Appleby? North Country, I suppose. My husband is from Shropshire; I'm from nowhere worth speaking of. This is Miss Busst. This is Mr. Rumsby. George is still far too fat, Mr. Hailstone. Don't bother about the people still in the boat. You'll meet them presently. You'll have a good time. We all have a good time."

"A good time," said Miss Busst with excessive decision. "That's it."

"Marvellous cooking," said Mr. Rumsby. "Mostly by Heaven himself. Marvellous swimming. Marvellous time." Mr. Rumsby's mouth dropped open and he stared at nothing in particular.

George sniffed.

"A good time *in every way*," said Miss Busst, a shade defensively. "There are a great many books. We hold a religious service on the first Sunday of every month. Sir

Mervyn gives an address. A most devout man; he assures me that at home he never missed a religious service in years."

"Ah," said Appleby. "But that was in jail."

Mr. Rumsby's mouth opened a shade wider; Mrs. Heaven gave a cheerless smile.

"Of course we all know about the man's misfortune. And we don't bring it up."

"You see, I am a police-officer and my mind rather runs on such things. At present I am interested in a murder which took place on this beach only yesterday." Appleby, thus triumphantly overgoing the forthright manner of Mrs. Heaven, looked easily from one to another. "Perhaps good times are confined to your strip of the island. Here are my friends coming down the beach. Two women and two men. You have room in your hotel?"

"We'll make it." Mrs. Heaven nodded briskly—she might well, Appleby thought, be the only brisk thing on the island. "And if you don't want a good time—well, it's not compulsory." She was looking from Miss Busst to Mr. Rumsby with a sudden sharp malice. "A good murder is no doubt more appealing to your type. I'm glad you've found one. It's not part of the room-service of our hotel." And abruptly Mrs. Heaven got into her stride again and moved to meet Appleby's companions.

It was all exceedingly odd; there was a protracted fuss of explanation and surprise during which Hailstone and George faded from the scene and Appleby withdrew a

little to take a compendious view of it. . . . Yes, it was
odd; yesterday a desert island and today a good time at
perhaps ten guineas a week. Yesterday murder and a deplorably empty sea; today any amount of queer fish for
the net. Yesterday a threatening perpetuity of tête-à-tête;
today a launch-load of over-age toast-golden Dianas and
the prospect of Sir Mervyn Poulish engaged in sabbatical
offices of pastoral care. But no doubt Hoppo would take
over that. . . . Appleby turned and walked further from
the group; walked until it was a splash of colour and jerky
movements against an emptiness of tropical beach and sky
and sea. The right proportions were before him now. He
shifted his ground until, close beside him, Unumunu's
grave served as a *repoussoir* to the scene. And there, then,
was the problem, with only the elusive savages as a missing
piece. The beach-suited embassy from Heaven's Hermitage Hotel; the veterans of the sun-deck café; the tracks of
a disappearing archaeologist and a superior dog: these and
a mound of sand. A problem, and one for which—uniquely
—he had to force himself to care. For it was provincial
and meaningless; a problem of the world-forgot, of the
vacuum into which they had been hurled by Hoppo's
whale. Hoppo's whales were on the high seas, they were
in the narrow seas and in the central sea. The war planes
were over Europe and Asia; their shadows cut the spires
of England, the mosques of Africa, the storied and fretted
temples of the East. The lights were out in Paris; in Pitts-
burgh they scarred the night to guide, at a thousand lathes,

the planet's biggest race yet; in Sydney, in Ankara, in Tokio hands were ready on the switch. Madness—but an action of magnitude and significance, a universal tragedy to which every human being stood in some moral relation, a great big fight directly and simply attractive to an unattached young man. . . . But here there was only the death of Sir Ponto Unumunu and the quaint dignity of a highly bred dog.

He walked slowly back. From the launch the Younger Crush were bathing; two frisky ladies had come on shore and were playfully pursuing a stout gentleman who flopped unbeautifully as he ran. Curious, Appleby reflected, that such an excessively un-Victorian way of life should have been foreseen by Edward Lear. But so it was:

> There was an Old Man of Corfu,
> Who never knew what he should do;
>   So he rushed up and down
>   Till the sun made him brown,
> That bewildered Old Man of Corfu—

the very core of Hermitage Hotel doctrine was evidently in the lines. . . . And suddenly Appleby's heart warmed to the companions of his adventures. For they were not like that. Diana, who had found that nightmare voyage full-time; Miss Curricle, who had braced herself to begin all over again at Eve; Glover, who had remembered the propriety of reading a proclamation; even old Hoppo, who in a last delirium had disputed with the Great Doctor on the foundations of the Anglican faith: they were out of a different drawer.

He was back where he had started and looking with a thoughtful eye at the paw-prints of the retreating George, at the brisk administrative capacity of the masculine Mrs. Heaven. . . . Yes, they were a different sort. One could make a team of them, if need drove.

11

Miss Curricle adjusted a deck-chair to the least lounging of its positions and sat down.

"The hotel is comfortable and clean," she said.

"Tolerably clean," said Mr. Hoppo.

"The hotel is comfortable and clean." Miss Curricle spoke with something like the semi-proprietorship of a man in a tourist office. At the same time her tone hinted at possible qualifications of the amenities described; the food might be indifferent or the guests undesirable. "Commonly I ask to be shown a room before booking. But in our present circumstances it would have been out of place. Particularly as Mr. Heaven is a somewhat unusual type to be proprietor of an hotel. I wonder what his history can be, and where he found such a wife? A gentleman, it seems."

"Perhaps," said Hoppo, "gentlemanlike would be the better description."

"I do not disagree with you. Possibly the son of a musician or painter of the self-made sort. His dress is not quite that of the gentleman. That diamond ring."

Colonel Glover looked up from a two-year-old copy of the *Times*.

APPLEBY ON ARARAT

"As a matter of fact, he claims to belong to the Shropshire Heavens. A bad hat, I suppose. He had to find himself a job, he says, being very much a younger son. And
I know they are a—um—prolific family."

"Perhaps a Seventh Heaven." Diana was looking happily into the depths of an enormous refrigerated drink.
"And now"—the joke could be seen dawning on her mind
in its full splendour—"he is Hoppo's Heaven. They're
ever such cobbers—pals, I mean."

"How we all wish that we had Mrs. Kittery's inex-
haustible wit." Hoppo gave a laugh in which whisky and
soda was just perceptibly operative. "Everything is so
vague here that I have been trying to sound him out. And
we have a common interest. We are both philatelists."

Diana's eyes rounded. "You didn't *seem* to be that when
we believed it was a desert island. And I didn't think
clergymen were allowed to be."

There was a moment's baffled silence and then, from a
corner of the veranda, Appleby chuckled. "Philanderers,
Diana. Philatelists are something quite different." He
turned to Hoppo. "Heaven collects stamps?"

Miss Curricle wobbled in her chair; Hoppo splashed
whisky on his borrowed shirt. For with the words
Appleby had given the effect of pouncing in the oddest
way—rather as a physician on holiday might pounce at a
glimpse of an intriguing rash.

"Yes, indeed. A most interesting collection. Ragged,
as almost any totally unspecialized collection must be

now-a-days. But with a number of remarkable things: a Moldavian Bull, for instance, and an Inverted Swan. And, although I cannot say he has a scholarly grasp of the subject—"

Glover rustled the browned and brittle *Times* with some impatience. "My boys used to collect stamps," he said. "But grown men—"

"One of the finest modern collections"—and Hoppo smiled as a man who plays a trump card—"was formed by the late King George the Fifth."

Appleby had risen and walked to the edge of the veranda. He looked down on the boat-house, the power-station, the spick-and-span out-buildings in their fresh, softly toned paints. "*All this, and Heaven too,*" he murmured. And then he frowned, for before him there had risen the picture of the thick smashed skull of Unumunu. Behind him his companions were restrainedly bickering; in front, in the middle distance, the hotel folk were splashing in the swimming-pool. And not many miles beyond, but made remote by more than a difficult climb, was the old encampment and the black man's grave.

"Comfortable and clean." Miss Curricle had gone back on her tracks. "Nevertheless I am with Mr. Hailstone and can well appreciate how he resents this intrusion. The dignity of science has always been appreciated in my family. Our dear father, though much burdened by the responsibilities of a senior civil servant, was always keenly interested. My maternal grandfather was acquainted with

Lord Kelvin."

Glover had put the *Times* over his face. His spare stomach rhythmically rose and fell.

"And so I can say with some confidence that Mr. Hailstone is the type of the true scientist. And just as he is on the verge, maybe, of an important discovery, Mr. Heaven arrives and builds his hotel for the convenience of pleasure-seekers and escapists—people *not* in a good tradition at all."

"Incidentally," said Hoppo, "for the convenience of ourselves. And on credit, too, more or less."

"No doubt. I do not question our good fortune. I merely assert that Mr. Hailstone—"

"Hailstone seems to me an uncommonly lazy fellow." Mr. Hoppo eased a cushion behind his head.

"I suggest that you confuse him with his dog. Of George I admit that I cannot approve. My dear mother—"

Appleby wandered out of earshot and into the hot sun. Somewhere the gramophone was again churning out a sad exclaiming dance-music with the senseless pertinacity of some fated machine for which the magic check has been forgotten. Old music still, infinitely dolorous, about the Valley of the Moon. *The vaaaley of the moooon . . . the vaaaaaly*— Abruptly the lugubrious strains ceased, as if, after all, the sorcerer and his word had returned. For a moment there were only the squeals and yells from the bathing-pool, a hullabaloo as of demoralized savages in rut; and then the gramophone, like some slick little time-machine, slipped back five years further and spoke of Valencia—spoke of Valencia over and over again. Valencia . . . *Valencia* . . . tum-ti tum-ti tum-ti *tum* . . . *VALENCIA.* Banal and calculated, the stuff trickled out of a futile past, worked on the gut, lapped up to the higher centres, sent a sticky and emotive spindrift over the very ramparts of the mind. Appleby took to his heels. There was the swimming-pool to pass and then he would have a chance of setting his wits to work. . . . "Ragged," he said to himself as he ran. "Ragged . . . no scholarly grasp." He frowned at a fat woman slopping past him in sandals. Probably a side-line, he thought. He dropped to a walk with the pool before him. "Hailstone must know a lot. If he can be spurred to utter."

Half-a-dozen people were grampusing about the pool, with more persistent activity of lungs than of limb. Until their own arrival at the hotel there could not have been many more than a dozen guests all told. But after the nightmare solitude of the ocean, the too-familiar society of the glade, the new faces had been as baffling as a stellar arithmetic. Now they had sorted themselves out. Over there by the drinks were the crafty features Appleby had recalled at once—Sir Mervyn Poulish's, the magnate who so sensationally went to jail after the sugar scandal. No doing of Appleby's, so social embarrassment need not result. And the fellow beside him who was being slapped and kneaded by the handyman Mudge—Jenner, his name—might well be his twin in polished rascality. The others, though they would not be approved of by the severe and gloomy body of men who compose His Majesty's judges, seemed not criminal in type. Appleby remembered in the old play the characters so excellently named Supervacuo and Lussurioso. That was about the size of them—as Miss Curricle said, *not* in a good tradition at all. But one could make a note that one might rely on Mudge. . . .

And there was Heaven himself, sufficiently odd to make an adequate companion piece to his grotesque wife. He was a man lank and then suddenly pudgy-faced, like a baby monstrously sprouted; filling the brief intermissions of his pretentious patter with involuntary and infantile sounds, as if he had never contrived through a long verbal development to shut down on his first efforts at speech. Appleby paused for a moment to observe him. His philately too, perhaps, was a sort of fossil from the past. But Appleby wondered.

"John!" It was Diana panting behind him. "Take me."

"I'm going away to think."

"I'll help. I did once, didn't I? When you said perhaps you ought to have taken out classes too?"

"You helped. It was a first gleam of light—or thereabouts. And we need more."

"It's all so vague, isn't it?" She had fallen into step by his side.

He smiled. "A general lack of definition is at present the keynote of the whole affair. But do you want to come?

I thought that now you had the run of a soda-fountain—"

"Listen." They stopped and the throb of the gramo-phone faintly reached them. "Something about a little jacket of blue. That all the sailors knew. It was going about five years ago when I was nineteen. When I got married. I can't bear it."

He looked at her curiously, careful still to know noth-ing of her history. "They're certainly mournful, old popular tunes."

"I feel blue again, John, myself. Just like on the liner." She surveyed the beach, the seeping sunshine, the water, the people idling—surveyed its familiarity, puzzled. "It ought to be alright—*all right*, I mean. It's like a little bit of Bondi. But I hate it."

"The war—"

"Yes, I know. And it's worse for a man." She looked at the person called Jenner who was being pounded by Mudge. "For a real man. But just the—the white man in the tropics is a bit blue. An island like this is for Ponto—for Ham. And now Ponto's not here. Only all these—these—"

"Japhets."

"Yes. And then—" she stopped. "But I'm getting in the way of your think. Is it about Ponto and the savages?"

"Certainly not about the savages."

"There's George." She pointed to an eminence on their right. And there certainly was George. In a patch of shade and from his favourite position of calculated repose he was surveying the pool with an extreme of gloom. But now he rose and came forward, his large black nose minutely working and his paws exactly clearing the ground as he moved. Diana fussed over him and he responded with the economical graciousness of royalty at a party. It was clear that George regarded the new-comers as distinct from the general run of hotel folk. All three moved on together.

"John"—Diana spoke with unusual deliberation— "there weren't any savages, were there?"

He stopped in his tracks. "How do you know that?"

"Just because of that time when I said there was a—a discrepancy. We thought of savages and cooking pots, and that might be right or wrong. But savages smuggling a body into the sea—"

"Quite so. Unumunu was killed in the jungle and his body hauled laboriously through its cover until just op- posite the spot where a current would carry it right away. It didn't *look* like savages. Still, I wasn't at all sure. Natives in some stage of demoralization or tribal disintegration might behave in that way—gratifying the instinct to kill on the quiet. But I doubted it and was impressed when Hailstone in his lackadaisical way plainly doubted it too. But there was another and much more conclusive fact. You remember the spear that landed in our table?"

"Yes. We all looked at it."

Appleby grinned. "But nobody smelt it but me. And I discovered that the flaming effect was secured with petrol

—nothing less. And savages haven't the knack of refining petroleum, as far as I know. I don't doubt that there are savages and that we may come on them yet. But everything that we encountered was a put-up job. No wonder we weren't all slaughtered."

From George, who had ambled into the undergrowth, there came an obscure noise. It sounded not unlike a chuckle. But perhaps it was a perfunctory display of belligerence against a lizard.

"I don't at all see that it's no wonder. Why should it be just Ponto that was to be slaughtered?"

"Perhaps it was to be all of us. Perhaps Unumunu was just dealt with first. But, you see, it became known that we were on the island, and a general slaughter—even if put down to visiting natives—might have been reckoned to produce an undesirable sensation or panic." He paused. "Take it in this order. You kill Unumunu and so arrange things that his body, forty to one, will float out to sea. Well, the disappearance of one odd black man may not create much fuss. But the body is found and it is evident he has been murdered; soon everyone will know. What, in a tiny community like this, is the best way to huddle the matter up? Somewhere within reach there are natives of doubtful habits. So make out that the black man was killed by them. Support this by the alarming but harmless nocturnal raid to which we were subjected. The story then is that some copper-coloured savages have killed a nigger and brandished a spear or two before decamping. Still no great cause for alarm—or even for curiosity in a lethargic place like this—but, at the same time, any wholesale elimination of us new-comers is no longer practicable at the moment. . . . Grant some motive for extreme measures at the beginning and it is all coherent enough."

Diana stooped to pluck an orchid. "I love the way you talk," she said. "The—the way your mind goes. It's like watching Don Bradman bat."

He was startled at the enormousness of the compliment. And he was suddenly aware of how far he was from home. The assistant-commissioner, restless and gloomy behind his desk, would not equate the elements of logic with the strokes of Hammond or Jack Hobbs.

"And now consider this. Was Unumunu just a beginning and the sequel abortive because the killer learnt that our existence had become generally known? Or was it just Unumunu whom it was necessary to dispatch? Do you collect Moldavian Bulls, or Hoppo's Inverted Hippos?" He grinned at her, pleased with this sudden transition to obscurity.

But Diana remained grave. "The stamp-collecting really means something? It's—it's relevant? You're not just throwing it in as trimmings?"

George had expended sufficient effort to get some way in front; he had turned and, planted on the path, was fixing Appleby with a censorious eye.

"I believe the stamps really to be an obscure sort of pointer. Not directly towards Unumunu but towards a general situation in terms of which his death may be explained. Have you noticed how slowly we learn any sort of why and wherefore about this island? How cut off are we; how often and how freely can people come and go; what has brought them here in their several groups; what of the past of each?" He peered into the impenetrable jungle. "All that."

"It's nice to think we're going to be busy. Groups? I suppose we're a group ourselves."

"Assuredly. It is still theoretically possible that we have brought our own serpent into Eden—or out of the Ark. Each of us had done a certain amount of solitary wandering. Think of Miss Curricle. She was away for the whole of the day on which Unumunu died, and she was still away when the savages appeared. What about her stage-managing it all? She has the instinct of showmanship; whatever happens there is a faint suggestion that she is pulling the wires."

"But the savages weren't—weren't puppets. She couldn't have been pulling *their* wires."

"The hotel has native servants of some sort, and so probably has Hailstone. She might have bribed them and worked the thing up. Any of us might."

"You're very"—Diana bent down and pulled George by the ear, rather as if he might prove to be a big woolly dictionary—"theoretical."

"I admit that the suggestion is probably quite academic. Still, we are Group One. And Group Two we are approaching now—Hailstone and his fellow diggers—and, of course, George."

"Diggers?" said Diana, for whom the word held another and national connotation. "Oh, I see. And Group Three is all the people at the hotel."

"Group Three is Heaven, whom we have hardly contacted yet, and Mrs. Heaven, and perhaps the organization of the place generally. And the dozen or so people at the hotel may be one group or several. . . . There's somebody coming."

George had stopped and was growling with force and conviction. And down the faintly marked path towards them came a lean figure in dirty ducks.

"He's wounded!" said Diana.

Appleby shook his head. "He's very drunk."

12

AGAINST A BACKGROUND OF WHEELING PARAKEETS THE
stranger lurched, halted, fixed upon them a bloodshot
eye. His hands fumbled for his trousers pockets, shot
futilely down his thighs, tried again, succeeded and disappeared. The new posture steadied him; he advanced
again in a tolerably straight line.

"Have a drink," he said.

They looked at him in silence, as one looks at something inevitable in a film. He was unshaven and his hair
hung lank down to his eyes; and as they looked he kicked
suddenly at air—kicked, perhaps, at some hallucinatory
George immediately before him.

"Have a drink," he repeated. And as he spoke—chal-
lengingly, this time—he half turned as if the means of im-
plementing the offer must be at his shoulder. The jungle
baffled him; he scowled at it, seemingly flogging on his
brain to work the thing out. "At the bungalow," he said.
"That's it. Come along." He turned about—it was another effort of the intellect—and moved in the direction
from which he had come, steadying himself to look elab-
orately over his shoulder every few yards. They followed, Diana pleased, Appleby as if with the pages of

forgotten Conrads flicking over uncomfortably in his brain. And George came discreetly in the rear.

"A sample of Group Two," Appleby murmured. "Another demoralized Japhet. No wonder they don't get much done. Good Lord!"

They had come abruptly into a clearing, and what the staggering figure before them had called the bungalow was revealed. More temporary-seeming than the hotel, it was also more pleasing to the eye. Light and shade flowed over it at the waving of palm tops high above; there was a small, carefully screened bed of English flowers in colours that were quaintly answered in trim and spotless veranda blinds. The whole thing was tiny—something to be carted round in sections—but it was decently proportioned and solidly made.

"Pretty," said Diana.

"Efficient. Aluminium paint on the roof. That glass cuts out heat. And look at the tanks. Traps to catch and reject the first flow from the catchment. Simple and means no dust in your water. But something I didn't see in—"

"No doubt. And we eat soap. Are we really going to pay a visit?"

"Certainly. This specimen must share with Hailstone. Up we go."

They climbed the veranda steps and found their host stumbling among wicker chairs. He grabbed one of these. "Will you all"—he paused and his brows contracted in an effort of calculation—"will you both sit down? Hail-

stone's rather been expecting some of you. My name's
Dunchue." He paused again and looked wearily amused.
"Dunchue. At school they called me—" His wandering
eye happened on Diana. "Get drinks," he said and disappeared.

Appleby laughed. "A poser for the Curricle. Not
gentlemanlike, but a gentleman. I wonder what they do
about gentlemen's gentlemen? Ah! What are called soft-
footed native boys." From the darkness of the bungalow
a youth—coppery, slim, timid-eyed—came gliding out
with a tray. "I wonder if this lad pitched one of those
spears? Never cease suspecting, Diana. It's our job. . . .
You have a lovely view."

Dunchue had returned and was painfully unstoppering
a decanter.

"View. Only distance could give any enchantment to a
view of this blud—this blasted island. That or a good,
honest-to-God dig. I'm beginning to think we'll never
begin. Bad enough before that filthy hotel. Those brats"—
he jerked a trembling thumb in the direction in which the
boy had vanished—"could be organized for any bit of
futile devilry. But set them to dig our site and they bolt.
Place is taboo—that sort of thing. And now that they can
get tucker out of Heaven and his beastly pub there's no
ordering them." He poured three glasses brim full and
handed them round. "I used to blame Hailstone for not
being in earnest. But I suppose the old bast—boy has tried
his best. Only I feel"—and Dunchue sat down, his face

suddenly oddly haunted—"I feel the place may get on top of us if we hang about much longer."

"It must be trying," Appleby said vaguely. He had taken a sip from his glass and was staring at it with puzzled distaste.

"I sometimes feel—" Dunchue paused and looked at them suspiciously—a man who wonders how much is apparent or guessed. "I sometimes feel as if I might lose my form altogether. Go—go to the devil."

"Yes, I see. Of course, even so, it might only be a visit. You'd be all right in another environment."

"All right—what the hell do you mean, all right? Is there anything wrong with me now?" Dunchue had jumped up, splashing himself. He stood trembling; he gulped down the remains of his drink and paced up and down the veranda, an incongruous figure amid its neatness. Suddenly he stopped. "My God!" he said, "I'm tight." His voice held just the surprise of a man who, in the heat of a battle, discovers that he has been wounded to the death.

There was an embarrassed silence. Diana had set down her drink; her mind was plainly turning to the soda-fountain she had abandoned. George was wandering about the veranda sniffing, rather as if puzzled by those other and hallucinatory Georges with which the bungalow was tenanted. From some outhouse at the back came the murmur of a native speech, soft, unaccented, ceaseless. It was Dunchue who spoke again.

"No good cutting out. The idea's too fascinating. And I believe myself, fantastic though it seems, that Hailstone's right. Of course you know that he's absolutely first-class"—Dunchue squared himself, suddenly the eternal assistant—"and, in fact, nobody can touch him since old Sempel died. So it seems worth hanging on. But he's a rum chap—genius often is." He reached for the decanter and drank again. "I sometimes think it's not just natural laziness with him, nor yet the climate. Look how he makes these black cattle keep this place. His idleness is an inhibition of some sort—psychologist's stuff." He drained his glass. "Like drink; something to do with your mother or your nurse."

Again there was a silence. Appleby, staring into the jungle, chose between a number of feelers he wished to put out.

"Those black cattle," he said; "you don't seem to care for them?"

"Hate all blacks—intensely boring. Hate the tropics—intensely boring too."

"But surely—" Appleby checked himself. "And Hailstone?"

"Same. Hates natives. Odd that he can manage them."

"Would you say that he hates blacks—of any sort—enough to hit a stray one on the head?"

"Might kick him on the—on the behind." Dunchue looked puzzled, and Appleby wondered if the Unumunu affair had not yet pierced the alcoholic fog around him.

"And I daresay might kill a man, might Hailstone. Has claws, you know, great Tabby that he seems. Absolutely first-class." Dunchue was becoming discernibly drunker.

"Kill a man over what? Money, women, political passion?"

"Good lord, no." Dunchue laughed the high, strained laugh of a man with a dry tongue and throat. "You don't know the old boy at all." He stopped laughing and his face clouded with a sort of dull suspicion. "What's all this, anyway? You talk like a damned policeman."

"As it happens, I am. And a man has been killed on the island. I'm going to find out how, even if it means stretching my warrant to cover a Crown Colony."

"Crown Colony? I'm not sure the island isn't American." Dunchue's interest was now perfunctory. "There's a British Governor somewhere about, I believe, but I'm not sure if he asks us to his levees. A man killed? Likely enough. Filthy place all round."

Diana was leaning over the veranda rail, as if scarcely listening to the talk. But now she turned round and looked full at Dunchue.

"Did you know Sir Ponto Unumunu?" she asked gravely. "He was an—an anthropologist too."

"I'm not an anthropologist. I'm an archaeologist. There's a difference." He scrubbed at his eyes, seemed to look at Diana for the first time. "Hullo! I say, will you have a drink? Got one? Don't think me meaning to be rude. Touch of fever the other day—leaves one a bit vague. Is that the man they've killed—Sir—?"

"Ponto Unumunu."

"No, never heard of him. Anthropologist? Sounds queer." Dunchue picked up the decanter and then thought better of it. "Hope you'll stay and lunch."

Appleby nodded cheerfully. "May we—and ask questions? I would like to know a lot about Heaven and his pub."

"Nasty chap." Dunchue stared inattentively at his visitors for some seconds. "But I *have* heard of him— Unumunu, I mean. Not as any sort of scientist, though, and that put me off. Heaven, of course—we can tell you something about him. Only I have heard of this Unumunu, but I can't think where." He set down his glass, and with the action turned instantaneously glum. "Not long ago." With his hair falling over one eye he stared at them in lethargic misery. "My mind's going." He began to cry.

Diana looked uncomfortable; Appleby, whom, of professional habit, the vagaries of human conduct had little power to disconcert, looked placidly into distance. And from somewhere in the interior of the bungalow came an ironical snuffle which was undoubtedly made by George.

"John"—Diana spoke cautiously across the blubbering man—"ought we just to drift off?"

He shook his head and waited. "Unumunu," he said presently. "An odd name. One would hardly forget it." He paused again. "And he was an odd chap too." He continued to talk placidly.

Below them blue sea lapped a beach which shimmered and vibrated in the sun; George had reappeared and sunk, all tongue and pant, beneath a chair; from inside came a slow chink of silver, as of a table being very slowly laid. Dunchue's eyes, still wet with tears, closed; his mouth fell open with a sudden, helpless, repulsive jerk; his body slumped as he sat. For some moments Appleby talked softly on; then he stood up. "I'm going to have a look round. Just mind the cradle." He slipped from the veranda into the half-light of the house.

Two native boys were working in a long narrow living-room which ran the length of the bungalow; they looked at him incuriously and without interrupting the slow and graceful rhythm with which they were preparing for a meal. The scanty furniture was of laminated and cellu-losed wood: pleasing stuff from Finland or Sweden which would unscrew and pack into a small crate; there was a gramophone with a bust of Beethoven; the only other ornament stood on a desk and was a great bronze bowl of evident antiquity, embossed with dragons in a swirl of foliage. Appleby collated this mentally with remembered exhibits in the British Museum and turned to the books which covered one of the end walls. Most were in Ger-man but many were in English; there were others in what was discernibly a variety of Scandinavian languages; there was a big collection of scientific papers in Dutch. Everything spoke of cultures thousands of miles away;

the room was an enigma public and exposed; all this would have been evident the moment he was invited inside.

The boys, chattering softly, had left the room and Appleby risked a rapid rummage at the desk. One deep drawer held a series of bound note-books, and every one appeared filled from cover to cover with neat archaeological notes and sketches. These Appleby examined at dangerous length, though a glance was sufficient to show that they answered to the general atmosphere of the room. The story was Nordic all the way. It was the world of the Sagas that had been transported to this lazy, faintly sticky tropical isle.

The other drawers were locked—all save a shallow one at the top. Here he paused over a curiously shaped pipe and a plain hermetically sealed tin. There was a slither behind him and he slid the drawer back just as one of the boys returned to the room. A banal, too familiar business this of furtive search; he slipped back to the veranda and took a deep breath of hot, still air.

Dunchue was still a comatose mess; Diana was a sort of answering study in healthy sleepiness; only George had revived—his chin a good inch from the floor and his moist nose, while twitching distaste of a fly, steadily directed down the bungalow path with its little bed of flowers. And presently round a corner came Mr. Hailstone's comfortable umbrella, tortoise-like as before and the focus for a swirling coronal of minute, brilliantly plumaged birds. The native boys ran out and took the umbrella exactly as

Hailstone passed into the shade. He removed his blue-tinted glasses; caught sight of the visitors and returned them to his nose as if for more careful scrutiny; removed the spotless panama instead.

"How do you do?" he said. "I hope George has been doing the honours of this simple place." He glanced at his assistant. "And, of course, Dunchue too."

Dunchue stirred uneasily in his chair.

"It seems necessary—or rather unnecessary—to be frank." Hailstone had turned towards Diana with something of the cautious effort of a liner being manoeuvred against a quay. "Dunchue is a capital fellow. Since Sempel's young man Oplitz was killed I really don't think anybody can touch him. Quite first-class and thoroughly abreast—always the difficult thing for us older men. But sometimes I think the island doesn't quite suit him. And I wholly sympathize. I am, as it happens, an energetic man myself—George and I share a virtual immunity to climatic conditions—but I know how it is. One just can't keep on one's toes. When we begin to dig I am sure it will be better. But at present, as you see, he drinks." Hailstone moved slowly to a table. "Which reminds me, will you have a spot?"

They declined spots, indicating the glasses they had conscientiously drained. Hailstone poured himself out a trickle of the concoction from the decanter and eased himself into a chair. "The question is: who is going to begin to dig? One says one digs, but of course one doesn't.

One employs diggers and all one has to do for the most part is to keep on imploring them to dig gently. Well, now, I collected some natives—" He broke off. "But I am afraid all this will bore you. Are you comfortable at the hotel? It is a great pity we cannot accommodate you here. I can't think that all those frivolous people—" He broke off again and this time his eyes momentarily closed, as if polite solicitude were a soporific as powerful as his assistant's drink.

"We are comfortable enough," said Appleby, "and have really been uncommonly lucky. And we are not at all bored. Your dig is the interesting thing on the island, it seems to me."

Hailstone's eyes opened again, almost abruptly. "I collected some natives at the last trading post and thought that the problem was solved. It would not even be necessary to urge them to go gently, as they were guaranteed to be quite without energy. Unfortunately I ought to have brought them from much farther off. The site is taboo, or the next thing to it. And when the hotel came and stole some of them away, of course it became more difficult still. However"—he nodded vaguely—"I have no doubt we shall manage something soon."

"Mr. Hailstone"—Diana turned upon the archaeologist eyes which almost equalled in roundness his own blue spectacles—"couldn't *we* dig? It would be great fun. Ourselves, I mean, and some of the people from the hotel."

"Ah." Hailstone's voice was wistful. "Some of the

hotel people did offer once. But it wasn't a success. They expected quick results. There was friction and the thing broke down. But now that we have fresh blood something might be possible."

"Talking of fresh blood," said Appleby, "I have news about Unumunu's death. Perhaps it wasn't savages."

"He's been saying perhaps it was you." Dunchue had abruptly awakened and sat up. He was grinning at Hailstone, seemingly perfectly alert.

"That I killed the mysterious Negro? Dear me, perhaps it is time that we all had luncheon." Hailstone clapped his hands lightly. "And Mr. Appleby can inspect our boys. For something like savages were certainly involved in that curious spear-throwing business. Perhaps they were bribed." He rose. "George, with luck there will be a terrapin steak. Come in, Mrs. Kittery, I beg. My dear Appleby, come in." He moved towards the door, chuckling. "I can quite see what you call a 'case.' I can even see that Dunchue has seen it. Did Sir Pongo—"

"Ponto," said Diana severely.

"Did Sir Ponto and I come to blows over Miss—Miss Curricle? No. Did he covet my umbrella and was I after his gold watch? Again no. But was I jealous lest the rival scientist should beat me to the secrets of our savage neighbours' ancestors? Yes—and again abundantly yes. Dunchue, I was defending the dig against another authority on Pacific anthropology." They had entered the living-room and Hailstone was waving an unwontedly animated hand round a scene not so unfamiliar to Appleby as he imagined. "You see?" he said. He chuckled happily, recollected himself to find Diana a chair, gave himself over to chuckling in earnest. "Mr. Appleby, you are a detective. And I challenge you. . . . Do you see?"

13

APPLEBY, IT SEEMED, DID NOT SEE; HE PEERED ROUND the living-room with the conscientiously suspicious eye of a rural constable at the beginning of a yarn of crime. And Hailstone was delighted.

"We have always been a little nervous"—he clapped his hands as a summons for the first course—"of letting people in. The hotel people, for instance, we have entertained only on the veranda, and perhaps it was resented during the period they were helping us to dig. Dunchue, who has a subtle mind, once suggested a little camouflage, but I felt that to be carrying secrecy too far. He wanted to buy up some junk from visiting natives: shields, smoked scalps, totem-poles—that sort of thing. And to plaster the place with it."

"It was a nasty idea." Dunchue was still very gloomy. "I detest lower races. *All* lower races." He stared morosely at his chief, much as if he suspected him of being a Hotten-tot. "But it would have been the efficient thing. As it is, we can't be sure the secret hasn't leaked out. Why we're letting *you* in on it I don't quite know."

"Do I understand," asked Appleby, "that you are not archaeologists at all? That you are something quite different? Blackbirders, for instance?"

"Blackbirders?" Diana set down her tomato juice and looked perplexed. "I haven't seen anything but parrots and humming-birds and gulls."

Hailstone laughed quite merrily. "Mr. Appleby's mind still runs on my stalking black men. Blackbirders in this part of the world are a sort of slave-traders. We should be bad at it; we have let the objectionable Heaven have several black boys for just nothing at all. No, I think we may fairly claim to be true archaeologists."

"We deal," said Dunchue, "with a world of the past. Deal with it."

"Come, come"—Hailstone spoke rapidly—"we are not really going to fall down on the job. Mrs. Kittery is going to help us dig; we shall deal with it yet." He set down his glass and looked round the table, summoning their attention as if some climax had come. "*Vikings!*" he said.

Diana, who had perhaps failed to take out the appropriate classes for dealing with this piece of information, looked blank; Appleby—quite deceitfully—registered a slow semi-comprehension.

"There can't have been any Vikings here," he said.

Hailstone began to eat rapidly, as if the meal had suddenly become a bore.

"We are going to show you. The barrow. The dig."

"Wouldn't you need," asked Diana, "more than one barrow?"

From beneath the table George snored; Hailstone, in

whom an almost active habit was visibly rising, laughed with great good humour. "My dear lady, the barrow *is* the dig."

"Where they buried people?" asked Appleby.

"Things," said Dunchue. "Have you ever seen Traprain? It is—or was—quite a sizeable hill near the coast in the Scottish lowlands. Actually, it proved to be a solid cache of treasure; they left it there to be called for. Only it wasn't called for until a thousand years or so later."

"Treasure!" Diana's eyes were like saucers. "You are treasure hunting? Who will it belong to?"

"We have to find it first. And its value to science will be far greater than any intrinsic value in gold and gems." Hailstone turned to Appleby and talked absorbedly, rapidly. "They loved green water. They were the first and greatest navigators in history. It's impossible to say where they didn't get to. And these fellows may have come round the Horn. Think of that: a long plundering contact with South America centuries and centuries before Pizarro! And then everything dumped here. You see why we want to keep it quiet? A sensation, a rush of expeditions—and quite probably a mess. Dunchue, get the maps. For years I had a wild theory. Then, in the Marquesas, I picked up a real trace . . ." And Hailstone talked on and on. Behind him the boys slid noiselessly. George slumbered on the floor.

Appleby listened with conscientious attention. "I'm afraid I'm no scientist," he said. "My mind runs on all the wrong lines. Presumably if what you suppose is true, the hidden stuff will really be immensely valuable? Are you sure your plans haven't indeed leaked out? This odd hotel which has so mysteriously followed you and established itself; are you sure it isn't cover for some sort of gang on your tracks. What if Unumunu had contacted it and recognized somebody—some sort of disreputable pirate in the archaeological way—who then found it necessary to kill him? It's a wild suspicion—but then that's my line."

Hailstone let drop a spoon with a clatter. "What an extraordinary idea!" He looked anxiously at Dunchue. "The hotel was a bit queer from the first, wasn't it? Heaven just turned up with a boat and builders, and then the guests came. A close lot they are, too. A ship comes in once in six months from lord knows where."

"By the way," Appleby interrupted, "what about your own communications?"

"We can't afford much. A trader is putting in to have a look at us early next year. Always supposing it's not torpedoed. Your idea about the hotel disturbs me; I've always distrusted Heaven."

"Heaven collects stamps. Or—better—is in possession of something like a collection."

"Indeed?" Hailstone looked puzzled. "Not an endearing trait. But scarcely—"

"The connection with torpedoes is obvious."

Diana, enrapt before a passion-fruit sundae, smiled happily.

"When he talks like that," she said in a proprietory way, "his mind is working." She spooned deep into the ice-cream.

"We are at war. For all practical purposes the whole world is at war. And lots of people will go a long way to get clear of it. The difficulty is money. No government is very willing to finance its more pacifically minded subjects, for instance, in a comfortable tropic isle existence. One can't walk into a bank and draw money or arrange credit for such a purpose. But various categories of people are let slip away if they take no wealth with them. Their services are not reckoned valuable and if they can represent that they are going to live on their aunts at Timbuctoo they can clear out. Hence a war-time boom in rare stamps: they are a sort of negotiable security that can be smuggled with the greatest ease. And hence, it is quite clear, Heaven." Appleby paused. "Or so I should have supposed. But the value of your possible find makes me feel there may be something more in it than that. He may have other sources of gain in mind."

Hailstone sighed. "Everything is becoming so complicated. It's all this war—do you realize what ruination it is for workers like us? Harvard, Tokio, Cambridge, Moscow, Berlin: can you imagine"—he hesitated, searching for an image—"can you imagine something as swift and complicated and exact as first-class tennis happening between all these? In every one of them men waiting for the flashing ball that represents the progress of their subject —waiting to return it with a new spin, an unexpected twist, back over the net? And now this imbecility, with people like Heaven stuffing their pockets with rubbishing stamps and"—his features beneath their blue glasses lit up with sudden humour—"and then disturbing policemen torpedoed on one's doorstep! But I am sure we ought to be grateful for Appleby. He has put us wise to a possible danger of which we had no suspicion at all. George, we must be on guard—and Dunchue too, of course." And Hailstone exerted himself to sign for Benedictine.

The coffee was excellent and worth lingering over, nor was there any disposition to do otherwise. The active mood to which explanations of the dig had moved Hailstone was apparently dissipated; George was sound asleep; Dunchue, considerably sobered by the meal, was applying himself to captivating Diana. Appleby watched this latter process with a deplorably absent eye; he sat back, let the Benedictine cap an excellent hock and listened to the sluggish lap of waves which had broken their force on distant reefs. The sound was like the impotent murmuring of hours and days which had lost their power to beckon and compel. And this image in turn worked obscurely on his mind, turned and checked in his mind like a key that feels for its wards. Often such a key turns once only and the intricate thought has to follow it through or be baffled for good. . . . Appleby looked through the flywire of a long low window at the wicker chairs and spotless chromium table and abandoned glasses where they had drunk the abominable *aperitif* favoured by Dunchue; he returned gratefully to Hailstone's liqueur and stared into a new world in its colourless and tiny deeps. There it was, he said to himself; there it all was —or nearly all. His eye went back to Diana and to Dunchue leaning towards her over a bowl of fruit. They were as spectral, as unconvincing as a half-told film upon which one has suddenly come from the light of day. In five minutes Dunchue would reform; his hair would be brushed and a crease would creep magically into his trousers. But in ten there would be a misunderstanding; he would be drunker than ever and grow a three-days stubble overnight; it would take a tornado and much opportunity for heroism to set things right again. And even in the final close-up he would look engagingly dissipated still; he would have a horrid line of finically trimmed moustache. And Diana, after being soaked to the skin and obliged to undress behind a screen which proved amply decorous in the end— Appleby blinked. He had almost solved a mystery—almost solved a mystery which as yet had scarcely declared itself—but the island was ready to enfold him in its languor still. He drained his glass and as he did so the *Swiss Family Robinson*, long grown tenuous and remote, dissipated itself finally in air. He took a cigarette and lit it and saw a greater classic form itself in the blue and slowly curling smoke. "Tusitala," he said suddenly.

Hailstone looked up, startled. "I beg your pardon?"

"Nothing. I was just remembering a name the natives in these parts gave to Robert Louis Stevenson. Because he was a great teller of tales."

14

THE UNDIG DIG, THOUGHT APPLEBY. THE DIGGER UNDONE.
. . . He roused himself to join in the leisurely bustle of
going out to inspect. A second umbrella was found for
Dunchue and Diana; there was a little picnic basket and a
thermos; it was all like a mild amusement planned to fill
a children's afternoon. Hailstone roused George with a
sequence of progressively urgent whistles—rather as
Montaigne's father roused the infant essayist with a cautious music—and the party made its way into the beating sun and the louder lap of the sea. Far out the intense
blue showed a single line of foam, as if on the impassive
face of ocean the odd procession raised a tiny smile. A
wandering wind brought a waft, a sob, a sickly and dying
fall of music through the groves; an echo uncertainly murmured it ahead. Hailstone, under the stress of his pedestrianism, was silent and appeared to meditate his breathing. Appleby took advantage of his abstraction to study
the topography of the place.

All this segment of the island's east coast was flanked by
that line of difficult hills which, from their first encampment, they had called the eastern range. On its lower
slopes the jungle seemed here impassable, and before them

as they moved south the uplands climbed steadily in formations which were increasingly rocky and forbidding until abruptly they swung east, and ended in precipices sheer above the sea—a Hebridean rather than a Polynesian effect. They were thus walking into a species of natural *cul-de-sac*. But before the termination of this, and across a narrow neck of land which now appeared on the left before them, lay a peninsula of low sand-hills and scrubby grass. It was towards this that they were making their way, with the bungalow now a quarter of a mile behind them and the hotel perhaps a mile and a half behind that.

Appleby looked at the uplands on his right. Beyond them could momentarily be seen the merest tip of the eminence they had called Ararat; perhaps, he thought, it had now better be renamed Spy-glass Hill. From there the range cut off any view of most of this narrow coastal strip; hence had arisen their first inability to distinguish any signs of habitation on the island. He looked back at the bungalow, planted amid palms where the range swept nearest to the sea. It occurred to him that it would be pleasing to have a revolver—the way they were going could so very patently be a trap. But things might not stand like that at all. . . . And his mind went back to consider the hotel and the shady sanctuary provided by Mr. Heaven there.

Shadowy and unimportant it had appeared hitherto— an odd and possibly rather shameful institution which served as a convenience until one could get away. But now, with things perhaps going to happen— He turned to Hailstone.

"This fellow Heaven," he asked; "he didn't bring his escapists all in one bunch?"

"I think they came in two lots. It is a comfort that the place now seems to be full—with yourselves more than full. They are a great nuisance." Hailstone spoke mildly. "And they seem to dislike George." His voice held rather more spirit.

"George scarcely seems disturbed."

"George is an exceptionally good-tempered dog. One of them—I think a man named Jenner—kicked him only the other day."

"Which lot did Jenner come with?"

Appleby's question had—oddly—the air of following logically upon what he had just heard. And behind his blue glasses Hailstone appeared to be staring absently out to sea; he might have been attempting an estimate of something new that suddenly confronted him.

"I believe," he said, "Jenner was with the second lot."

"Did you get the impression that the second lot were in any way unexpected?"

Hailstone stooped to pluck grass seeds from George's untropical fleece. When he spoke it was in a voice that was frankly disturbed. "You really think—?"

"It seems not improbable that there are people at the hotel who have designs against you." Appleby in his turn paused to stare far across the ocean. "How Unumunu's death fits in I don't at all know. But when the picture becomes clearer it will find its place. Meanwhile we must be cautious. But I doubt if there is cause for real alarm."

Appleby spoke with a cheerfulness which he was suddenly far from feeling. It disturbed him to be told that the man named Jenner had kicked George.

A gull wheeled overhead; its swift shadow cut the sand like a summons to act. And the dig Appleby felt he would willingly take for granted at the moment; he wanted to get back and, for the first time, really look at Heaven's hotel. What sort of a rascal was Sir Mervyn Poulish, the defaulting financier? That was important. Was he right in his estimate of Mudge, the only white servant? That was important too. And about Heaven himself—

"About Heaven." Hailstone's voice cut startlingly in on his thought. "The more I think about him the more troubled I am. This stamp business you have so brilliantly spotted: surely it can't all be based on that? I can see that there may be a handsome profit if he has the means of disposing of the things again one day. But banking on the world being busy stamp-collecting in the later twentieth century—" He shrugged his shoulders, so that the shadow of the umbrella gave a little jump before them. "I believe he's up to something else." He was silent for some minutes; they were now plodding laboriously over soft sand. "Somewhere—right at the beginning—Dunchue may have talked; he was drinking long before we came here, I am sorry to say." He paused again. "The dig *is* a prize, you know—in the mere piratical way. There may be untold gold." He was looking at Appleby, perhaps distrustfully, through the cold blue of his glasses.

"I certainly believe that Heaven is interested in more than stamps."

Hailstone sighed. "I am used to an enigmatic attitude. George has something of it. . . . Ah, here we are."

A Brobdingnagian child, playing patty-pans amid these low sandhills and armed with something the size of a cinema, might have turned out just such a memorial as Hailstone's barrow. It loomed above and before them, a vast severe cube of sand and tussocky grass, the absoluteness of its geometrical form scarcely eroded by time. Diana cried out, like a tourist when the coloured lights are switched on in the cave; Appleby stared at the thing, perplexed.

"You could play cricket on it," he said.

Hailstone laughed. "We have never thought of that. But it's a big proposition, as you see. One begins to feel like the rat gnawing at the mountain."

"But surely they can't have buried all that? It would require a modern liner—"

"There was a little fleet, I suspect." Dunchue was looking at the barrow like a lover, and now turned from Diana for the first time since they had set out. "But it's as big as you see it because for some reason it has steadily accreted sand. Particularly on top—and yet always keeping its own form. Something to do with the binding action of winter grasses, Hailstone thinks." He shook his head, with one of his intemperate transitions into gloom. "Impacted, too, after a little way. Getting to the stuff will be like burrowing through a pyramid."

Diana looked dismayed. "You mean the treasure's very far inside?"

"Far enough inside to make a steam shovel desirable. Not even Hailstone getting us all on our toes, George included, is likely to make short work of it." Dunchue sat down and, as if for want of a better object, began to excavate the picnic basket.

"George," said Hailstone mildly, "is doing his best." And this was true. It was evident that the vast and unaccountable object, so severely angular amid the lush and convoluted life of the island, presented this monstrously lazy dog with an irresistible intellectual stimulus. He had bounded off to the barrow with a yelp and was absurdly scratching at the nearest of its massive bastions. "I often remark that George is an example to us all."

"Couldn't you blow it up?" asked Diana.

"Conceivably we could." Hailstone looked slightly shocked at the question. "But unfortunately we are quite without explosives. And one couldn't tell what damage one might do to fragile and crumbling objects inside. Would you care to climb to the top? There is an easy route from the other side."

Leaving George to his futile labours, they climbed. The
barrow, Appleby saw, was very near the ocean's edge;
one could look down on deep water almost immediately
below. But this was not the observation of most immediate interest to be made. For planted in the centre of the
sandy plateau on which they now stood, and applying
himself to what had every appearance of being a bottle
of champagne, was his host of the hotel. Like the saints
in the hymn, they had toiled up to Heaven. But if there
were golden crowns to gain it appeared to be the hotel-
keeper who had an eye on them. Beside him on the sand
lay a formidable spade.

He rose as they approached, and Appleby scrutinized
him more carefully than before. His head moved uneasily upon his shoulders and his features worked uneasily
about his face—a moon of a face that matched his lank
body no better than a shuddery polyp accidentally impaled upon some spider-like creature of the deeps. And he
advanced upon them to an accompaniment of little, in-
choate, involuntary sounds—a strange mooing as of beeves
on distant pastures, or thunder infinitely remote, or swallows in the great chimneys of an ancient house. He advanced thus and with his eyes screwed up against the
light—unprepossessing, affected, perhaps formidably intelligent. With a hand from which there gleamed a large
diamond he swept his topee from his head—and far away
across invisible valleys the cattle lifted their heads and
bellowed to the breeze; he bowed to Diana and spoke to

the new-comers at large.

"A delightful eminence from which to take the air. Mrs. Kittery, gentlemen—a glass of wine?" High up the swallows wheeled and twittered amid the crumbling stones.

Dunchue set down the picnic basket once more—but this time rather as if he were preparing for a fight. Hailstone planted his umbrella like a standard in the sand. George, appearing breathless from his burrowing, growled a new growl—a growl disconcertingly like cattle mooing beyond a shadowy horizon. And for a moment Heaven's confidence flickered; his face twitched into uneasy smiles, his head jerked on his shoulders, his free hand made indecisive gestures before his chest. And then like a watery lightning a snicker and chuckle sounded through the far thunder; his eyes screwed up farther and glinted darkly from some hidden depth of malice and power. He was laughing at them. And then he turned and lifted from its little ice-box the bottle of champagne.

"You will take wine with me?" he repeated—and stood suave and slightly twitching before them.

"Thank you, we have our own provision." Hailstone spoke with his wonted mildness. But he was standing very upright beneath the umbrella—determined to get on his toes, Appleby thought—and it was a poise which held its own affectation. For Hailstone was fundamentally not rigid or upstanding; despite the efficiency of his bungalow his languor was real—real or based on the reality of something supple, devious, pliant in his nature. *Parendo vincitur*, thought Appleby. And he remembered that on Unumunu's beach it was something ambiguous about Hailstone by which he had first been struck. But at least the man was bent on giving a very different impression now; he was standing up to this queer creature from the hotel with all the directness of a Colonel Glover.

"Mr. Heaven," said Hailstone, "may I ask what you are doing on this tumulus with a spade?"

"This tumulus?" Heaven's head lunged queerly on his shoulders; it was the motion of a cow obeying an attenuated instinct to butt, and the likeness was enforced by a faint mooing as he peered innocently about him. "Can I have strayed across your dig? I am exceedingly sorry, my dear sir. And as for the spade"—the snicker interpolated itself again between Heaven's syllables—"I am afraid that it is employed in the service of the stomach rather than of the mind. Edible worms, Mr. Hailstone; we had hoped this evening to serve an entree of edible worms. A delicacy very little known outside a restricted gastronomical circle." Heaven snickered and mooed, as if this palpable fantasy pleased him very much. "And found exclusively in the south seas. I found them mentioned in a curious treatise by Pierre Colet, for many years chef to the French Governor of New Caledonia. One digs quite deep in the sand—" And with another snicker and snigger Heaven thrust the spade deep into the surface at his feet.

The gesture was something between a mere impertinence and a manifesto. Dunchue, who had been glowering in the background, took it for the latter. He strode forward, and it was evident that to cope with a situation such as this came more naturally to him than to his chief.

"This barrow," he said evenly, "is of great importance to something called Pacific archaeology. It may help us to sort out the movements of all the peoples of the Pacific basin. We are not going to let it be interfered with by rubbishing people hoping to fill their pockets from some non-existent treasure. You understand me?"

He was glaring at Heaven, and Heaven smiled, twitched and produced several new varieties of inarticulate sound. Angry sound, Appleby reflected—and kept a watchful eye for the man's next motions with the spade. But Heaven presently spoke as from a mood of considerable amusement.

"Do I understand, Dunchue, that you claim an exclusive legal proprietorship of this part of the island?"

"There is no law on the island. For that matter, there is lawlessness; a stranger was murdered here only the other day—and Mr. Appleby here is going to ask the reason why. We shouldn't care to overburden him with homicides." Dunchue took a further step forward. "But law here is for resolute men to make. This dig is ours. And if you interfere I promise that you shall never dine on worms again. The boot will be on the other foot." And Dunchue's harsh laughter rang out over the sand-hills.

Diana had sat down and was watching the warming-up

of this scene with wide-eyed satisfaction; it was clearly not such situations that tended to make her feel blue. She was looking at Dunchue with what Appleby—his mind straying momentarily to irrelevancies—felt to be distinctly facile admiration. Nevertheless he was not disposed to step into a prominent role himself. Instead, he sat down too and fell to tickling George's ear with a straw. George made indecisive noises, perhaps tentatively trying out a snicker of his own. Hailstone altered the pitch of his umbrella, as if feeling that the temperature on top of the barrow might be lowered that way. For seconds the whole scene hung in air, with no obvious sequel in sight. And then Heaven turned and walked back to the spot where they had first discovered him. The swallows flew up out of the chimney and were gone.

But the interview was not over. They saw him stoop, pick something from the ground and advance upon them once more, his features working jerkily, like a series of photographs rapidly flicked over by a thumb.

"No malice," he said; "we must not let Mrs. Kittery and Mr. Appleby suppose that there is real malice in our little community." With a wary eye on Dunchue he was yet enormously amused; his whole body now jerked and rolled with his head, threatening to spill a little pile of paper-covered sandwiches which he balanced before him with the hazardous agility of a performing seal. "A fairly sound caviar; perhaps you will let me add them to your own store?" He snickered and mooed. "As an *amende*, you understand, for meddling with—did you say Pacific archaeology?" He held out the packet to Hailstone. "Or shall I pass it on to Mr. Appleby?" He began to unwrap the sandwiches. Nobody spoke. He stopped. "Well well, it appears to be a case of caviar to the general. Perhaps we shall meet tomorrow, some of us, in a more composed mind."

Heaven bowed to Diana, turned round, gathered up his belongings and moved away. And as his head dipped below the barrow the swallows were silent, the cattle gave themselves to rest, the faint thunder faded on the air.

"Curious," said Appleby, as he and Diana walked back to the hotel. "Curious about that caviar. Do you remember the black spot in *Treasure Island?* It was something like that—notice to the enemy of what's coming to him. And I suppose you might describe caviar as the black blob. Heaven hands Hailstone the black blob. Curious, indeed." He spoke spasmodically, his glance moving restlessly over the beach before them.

The tide was withdrawing, leaving behind it a fresh myriad of tiny shells and, interspersed among these, thousands of dun fibrous balls of varying sizes—a barren fruit of the sea tumbled out as earnest of the bizarre world of the Tonga Trench. One of these Diana stooped like Atalanta to gather as she moved; light as thistledown and as solid looking as a tennis ball it lay in her hand.

"It wasn't only caviar sandwiches," she said carefully;

"it was sandwich-paper too. Perhaps what he was threatening to pass on to you was that. Not so much black spot or black blob as blackmail. You could have your sandwiches ready wrapped up in some threatening paper—"

He had stopped and was looking at her with honest admiration.

"Did you see the paper? I didn't spot anything unusual about it."

"I saw the edges. It looked like a good sandwich paper —rather thick. But yellower. John, it might have been something *old*. The stuff called—"

"Parchment."

"Yes. An old document, a plan, a—a chart."

He laughed—but not with much satisfaction. "*Treasure Island* again. And it *is* that. Jack and Ernest and the good pastor are out of date." Again he looked restlessly about him. "I wish I could see that conveniently impregnable stockade. I wish we could dump you in an apple-barrel, Diana, and really hear what's what." He shook his head. "But an old chart doesn't fit, all the same. . . . One could have a tropical version of a snow fight with these." He kicked one of the largest of the fibrous balls vigorously towards the sea.

"I should have thought an old chart was just right." Diana was disappointed. "But, if it worries you, do you think it would be possible to—to extort it from Heaven? I shouldn't imagine he has much guts."

"Perhaps not. And I daresay we could. Only the situation is rather delicate, isn't it? Here we are living on credit in his hotel, and with only the vaguest notion of when we shall get away."

Diana nodded sagaciously. "Yes," she said, "perhaps it's not just the time to give him the works. He has a yacht, it seems, but nobody knows when it's likely to be coming back. . . . And that reminds me. Something Dunchue said I was to tell you. Something he had remembered, he said, after all. About poor Pongo. Ponto, I mean." She looked momentarily contrite. "How quickly one forgets about people when they're dead."

"What did Dunchue remember?"

"Not much. When Heaven's yacht was in, the captain asked Dunchue on board. They had a great big radio— what nobody has here—that could pick up ordinary stuff from all over the place. And he remembers something about Ponto Unumunu from Cape Town. He can't remember what, but he thinks it was something to do with Kimberley. . . . Is that a place?"

"Yes." Appleby pursed his lips as if in half a mind to whistle. "Anything else?"

"Only that he only remembers at all because of something about somebody."

"Dear me."

"It does seem vague. He rather thinks it was that desperately wicked-looking man at the hotel. Poulish—Sir Something Poulish. He seems to remember that when there was this about Ponto Unumunu on the radio the man Poulish—who was there too, you see—was upset. And that's all he remembers. It's very little, isn't it?"

Appleby shook his head. "I can almost see it as being a shade too much. Particularly when I reflect on George."

"On the hound of the Hailstones?"

He nodded and walked on some paces. "You may think of George," he continued gravely, "as the merest decorative flourish—something to patter quaintly through the interspersed vacancies of our ragged adventures. Nothing, Diana, could be more fatally mistaken. Saint Francis preached to the Georges—but this George holds sermons for *me*." He looked at her and burst out laughing. "The Duke of Monmouth was betrayed by his George—it was in his breeches pocket, they say—but this George—"

"John, I think you in-insufferable. I don't know anything about the Duke of Monmouth. But if he carried a dog in his breeches pocket I think it was most unaristocratic and smelly."

And Diana dived at the littered sea-fruit at her feet and pelted him. But Appleby, heedless, was shouting with laughter—a strange behaviour in a policeman even when he feels himself on a trail, and one to be accounted for only by the stimulus of an exotic environment. And then he was striding rapidly ahead. "Diana"—most unjustly he called back over his shoulder—"stop fooling around. There's work to do." He moved on, stopped, waited—

and she found him looking at the island with eyes almost as round as her own would go. "And I'm hungry. I could even eat those bonzer worms." He was laughing at her again, and as happy as if the world were suddenly young. "Too right, Diana—I could. Too right."

15

Mr. Mudge, the handyman of the Hermitage Hotel, had a hut of his own on a slight eminence above the native servants' quarters. This made possible a surveillance to which, as a duty, he did not appear to take kindly—or so Appleby conjectured from his conversation when visited before dinner that evening. Mudge was preparing to immerse himself in a shower; he removed a white coat and looked dubiously at his visitor until assured that there was no ceremony; he began to remove a singlet and interrupted the operation to shake a gloomy head.

"No morals, Mr. Appleby," he said, "no morals at all." He shed the singlet and revealed a chest on which was tattooed a sort of popular version of the Medici Venus. "Lecherous as monkeys, sir—and none of the ways you'd think to stop them is any good whatever. Over there's a kind of dormitory for the gels, sir, and on the other side one for the lads. It worked for a time, and mighty surprised and sulky they were. But now"—he thrust his torso beneath an impending bucket and groped for a string— "well, irrelevant would be the word, sir, if you follow what I mean."

{ 155 }

"Ah," said Appleby.

"And no idea of monogamy, Mr. Appleby—none at all. With the visitors, of course, one expects that sort of thing. But when the natives turn out as bad or worse—well, sir, it begins to prey on the mind. Makes one think, if you follow me, Mr. Appleby."

"It does, indeed," said Appleby. "Let me pull that string."

"Thank you, sir. Slow and steady, if you will be so kind. We had a bazaar for Moral Welfare a little time back—but it didn't go through in the right spirit, I'm sorry to say." Mudge turned round and revealed across his spine what might have passed as an incident in the story of Daphnis and Chloe. "The truth is, Mr. Appleby, that tropical residence relaxes the moral fibres. Stern and true and tender is the North. With the South it's different. And never the twain should meet. You'll excuse a taste for the poetic, sir. It seems to come natural to a contemplative man. Would you ever have read Wordsworth's *Excursion*, now?"

"Yes."

"I'm delighted to hear it, Mr. Appleby. There's a great deal of contemplation there. I often take it down of an evening. But nobody else on the island seems to know it. I hope we may have some conversation, sir, from time to time. Would you ever have read Blair's *Grave*?"

"I'm afraid not."

"Ah." Mudge was disappointed. "Or Young's *Night*

Thoughts? Very meditative, Mr. Appleby; very meditative indeed."

"No—or only bits in anthologies."

"Well, they're at your service on the shelf, sir, at any time. And I'd venture to say that if you relish the *Excursion* you couldn't go far wrong with the others. A comfort, I find them, in our present restricted society. Thank you, Mr. Appleby, the striped towel."

Daphnis and Chloe, and the delicately posed Venus, were vigorously rubbed in turn. Appleby let a minute pass before asking: "Are they all of a piece, Mr. Mudge —the white folk, I mean? That moral fibre: is it about equally relaxed all round?"

This was a nice question which Mudge clearly relished.

"Well now, I think it's a matter of residence, as I say. Not that they don't all arrive from the start with equally frivolous ends, Mr. Appleby—no apprehension that life is earnest, none at all. But somehow there's a bit more sense to them when they first land than later on. Take Mr. Jenner, for instance."

"Ah," said Appleby quickly. "The man who kicked George."

"No doubt, sir. Well, Mr. Jenner hasn't been so long here as some; he came with the second lot. And I would say there was sense in Mr. Jenner."

"He does sensible things? Talks sensibly?"

Mudge shook his head. "No, Mr. Appleby, I wouldn't say that. Nothing so extreme as that, sir. He just looks

as if he might have something sensible in his head, if you
follow me."

"I see." Appleby's expression had grown sombre. "He
might be a man of rational purpose, whereas the others
seem to be without any plan for themselves?"

"Just that—and very choicely put, sir, if I may say so.
But I wouldn't confine it just to Mr. Jenner. There's one
or two others of the second batch that one has the same
feel of. To speak figuratively, Mr. Appleby, they might
have something up their sleeves—something more, that's
to say, than ignoble ease. Not natural-born lotos-eaters;
not just the kind to choose the cycle of Cathay. Having a
taste for rhyme, Mr. Appleby, you will catch the allu-
sions."

Appleby had begun to fill a pipe with Mr. Heaven's
excellent tobacco. Now he put it away.

"Mr. Mudge," he asked abruptly, "are you an honest
man?"

Mudge looked unoffended; he also looked doubtful.

"It's really hard to say. On earth the broken arc, Mr.
Appleby; one can't speak with complete conviction of
one's own moral nature. But, guardedly speaking, I should
say Yes."

"And well-affected to His Majesty the King?"

This time Mudge was startled—but emphatic.

"Decidedly, Mr. Appleby. I might define my position
as royalist in politics—very definitely so. And might I
ask—"

"We keep doubtful company here, Mr. Mudge, and ought to be sure of each other. I shan't say more at present. But believe me I'm not taking up your time just out of curiosity. And I have one or two more questions to ask —do you mind?"

Mudge slipped the Daphnis, the Chloe, the Venus beneath the cover of a fresh singlet. His features when they emerged from this operation were round-eyed and eager.

"Mr. Appleby, I think there may be profit in this. Anything you like."

"First, then, how did you hitch up with your present employers?"

"It was at Pago-Pago—and it happened because the mate of the tanker I had been on was a philosophical man."

"Indeed?"

"Yes, Mr. Appleby, a man of philosophical inclinations. We used to discuss metaphysical problems together from time to time. Only his position, I am sorry to say, was very unsound—very unsound indeed, Mr. Appleby. A solipsist, neither more nor less. Believe me, nothing would convince that man that anything existed outside his own head. At times it made me fair wild. Until one day, sir— and in the heat of argument, you will understand—it occurred to me that there could be no better argument than some sudden and acute physical stimulus from without."

"I see."

"He took it badly, I am sorry to say; he said he had never been kicked by a quartermaster before. So at Pago-

Pago I left the ship in somewhat irregular circumstances. Perhaps awkward circumstances wouldn't be too strong a phrase. And then I met Mr. Heaven. The hotel had been built then, and he was collecting his guests."

"Where from—and in what way? Do you know?"

But Mudge, for an intelligent man, knew surprisingly little. It appeared that he had just then come into possession of Dr. Armstrong's celebrated poem *The Art of Preserving Health*, and that he had accepted a job and subsequently sailed with the Heavens in an abstraction occasioned by a concentrated perusal of this masterpiece. And like many men of poetical or philosophical inclination he had little awareness of money; on the finances of the Hermitage Hotel and its guests he had only the vaguest ideas. But it was clear that the privilege of residence must be costly; the place had been put up with labour and materials brought from a great distance; somewhere Mr. Heaven supported a yacht; the number of guests envisaged had originally been very small.

Appleby seized on this last point. "Smaller than now —I mean without Colonel Glover and the rest of us? There was a second batch of people—do you think they were not originally reckoned upon?"

"I don't think they were entirely a surprise, Mr. Appleby. It was just, perhaps, a bigger recruitment than the Heavens had expected at the time."

"I see. And including Jenner, who kicked George and is not a natural-born lotos-eater. Now, Mr. Mudge, an-

APPLEBY ON ARARAT

other thing. About Sir Mervyn Poulish. Once, when the
yacht was in, Sir Mervyn happened to be on board when
a radio program from Cape Town announced something
about a Sir Ponto Unumunu and Kimberley. It disturbed
him. Does that mean anything to you?"

"Nothing at all, Mr. Appleby."

"I hardly expected it to." Appleby had turned round
and was looking out across the swift tropical dusk.
"There's something horribly unprotected about that
hotel."

In a line of windows before them lights were going up
behind the fly-wire and glass; at the farthest of these a
fat woman, partially dressed, could be seen dabbing
powder on her neck; the eye, shifting a fraction from this
prosaic exhibit, fell on a stealthily encroaching wilderness
of creeper and fern—a confusion of sombre and vivid
greens now blending into a single dark background for
scarlet flowers which, like opening wounds, grew more
clamant as they looked. Above, the palms had shed their
contours and flattened themselves against the sky, fragile
as silhouettes from the scissors of a Georgian lady which
the turn of time has thrown against some vast construction
of dully polished steel. Two stars came out. The mind,
tirelessly contriving its fictions, announced them as points
defining a straight line—but they were indeterminate
messes without relationship to each other save in terms
of some third thing at some one time. The sound of the
sea was alien and discouraging; the crickets were allies in

whose impotence one's own fate could be read. Swiftly the shadowy curtains of night fell; the island withdrew like a dancer within her veils; there was only the fat woman wriggling upwards into a dress and, far away in Hailstone's bungalow, one light burning.

Appleby, framed in the doorway to take his leave, turned round.

"What about prose, Mr. Mudge? Did you ever read *Treasure Island?*"

"No, Mr. Appleby, I can't say that I did."

"A few honest men and a boy found themselves on an island like this with a pack of rascals. They had to fight it out. Only first there was the job of getting quite clear who were rascals and who were honest men."

Mudge, slipping on the white coat in which he would presently direct the serving of dinner, paused to digest this literary intelligence.

"I suppose," he asked, "the rascals would have a ringleader?"

"They had. He was called Long John Silver."

"And here, Mr. Appleby, there would be a ringleader too? And perhaps you know who he is, though not who all his followers are?"

"Yes."

Mudge sighed. "There are great disadvantages in the meditative temperament, sir. It prevents one from getting up with things as quickly as one should. Might I ask how you found out?"

"I'm not sure that I can tell you. Yes—it was something that happened on a table. . . . You and I must keep an eye on each other. Good night."

And Appleby went out. From the Hermitage a xylophone was summoning softly to whatever Mr. Heaven had substituted for edible worms. Although, hours before, Appleby had told Diana that he was hungry, he ignored the call now; reaching the hotel, he walked to a far corner of the veranda from which he could look out to sea. The night was chilly, as the island nights were. But there was something else to it, he thought, tonight—a breath, a tremor that the weatherwise might read. Before him, the ocean was only an uncertain, glimmering floor; the intellect alone knew it as estranging and vast. And he looked out over it gravely, as one who searches for a definite and significant thing.

There was a step behind him and he turned to see the glow of a cigarette, the glimmer of white evening clothes, the sardonic features, faintly and dramatically lit from below, of the ruined financier, Sir Mervyn Poulish. The man spoke—indifferently, with the casual courtesy of a liner's deck. "Had any good fishing?"

Appleby shook his head. "No," he said. "Not yet."

16

"THE POINT," THOUGHT APPLEBY, LOOKING ROUND THE Hermitage dining-room, "is that probably I gave myself away. The tempo of the affair may now be governed by that. Perhaps a couple of hours more of the Appleby manner, and the affair will begin to conduct itself to a different tune. Meanwhile, best make talk while the electricity shines. For it may very well go out."

He looked about the dining-room again and realized that it bore an unfamiliar air. Mr. Heaven, in fact, had arranged what he called a *divertissement*. Appleby, who was not among those who relish expecting a dinner and finding a *divertissement* instead, surveyed the scene with a gloom not unworthy of the hound of the Hailstones itself. The usual tables had gone and in their place stood a great many small ones laid for two. On entering the dining-room one was given the end of a tangled silk ribbon; this Ariadne-like thread one followed until partnered with the particular Minotaur with whom one was expected to dine. It was, presumably, just another way of having a Good Time. And it had set Hoppo opposite the leader of the Younger Crush, Miss Busst; Miss Curricle opposite the vapid Mr. Rumsby; and Colonel Glover

opposite Jenner, that exemplar of a superior purpose
whose only recorded activity was the kicking of George.
. . . Appleby took the end of his ribbon. Sir Mervyn
Poulish, who had come in behind him, did the same. As
they were the last to arrive and only one table stood
vacant, the situation was clear. Nevertheless some sheep-
ish deference to the Spirit of Good Times induced them
to make a show of following their ribbons. It meant,
Appleby noticed, a sort of dance. He turned to Poulish.
"Did you ever," he asked gravely, "give yourself away?"
And he moved off across the room.

This adherence to the rules of the game was approved
by the seated guests. They met again in a far corner amid
some applause. And Poulish, apparently, was uncertain
of what he had heard. "I beg your pardon?" he said.

"I asked if you had ever given yourself badly away. I
have—only today. Excuse me." He retreated, hauling in
as he went.

They neared each other again in the middle of the
room. Miss Curricle, Appleby noted, was taking out her
divertissement in fixed glances at inanimate objects around
her; Hoppo was the wise man who submits to innocent
folly with a good grace; Glover looked badly in need of
a copy of the *Times*. And here was Poulish again. "Or
did I?" asked Appleby. "Did I perhaps manage to cover
myself up? You know the feeling. And policemen get it
very badly at times. Ah, here we are."

Their table was before them and they sat down, Poulish

with a doubtful eye on his partner.

"I suppose," said Appleby, "the idea is good." He indicated the paired diners around them. "Interchange of information . . . points of view . . . that sort of thing."

"Yes." There was a silence and Poulish added morosely, "Jolly good fun."

"Quite so." The table, Appleby noticed, was laid with hammers, chisels and saws. And in the middle, like a sword between Poulish and himself, was an enormous loaf about four feet long. He took up his saw and fell to work on it.

"I say"—Poulish spoke almost nervously—"I don't think you're meant to do that. It's a sort of joke—like sometimes on ships. In a minute a boy will come and take all this away. Then there'll be something decent to eat."

But Appleby, who had successfully cut through a large segment of the loaf, began to munch.

"A joke? I don't agree with you. I suppose this loaf to be a symbol. The bread of idleness. An element in the celebration of a sort of lily-livered mass. My own feeling is that even a black mass is preferable to that."

Poulish had darkly flushed. "We are some of us not here entirely of our own accord. Yourself, for instance."

"No doubt." Appleby munched again, with a sudden satisfaction not perhaps occasioned by the quality of the bread. "There are more reasons than one for seeking a hermitage, I don't deny." He looked round the room. "Would you be at all interested if I told you that many of these people are not where they think they are?"

Poulish took some seconds to consider this. "I should be rather pleased," he said. There was another silence, while they parted—Appleby somewhat reluctantly—with the hammers and saws. "What was that you meant," asked Poulish suddenly, "about giving yourself away?"

"I was confessing a habit. And I'm going to do it again. Let's talk about Cottonreels."

"About *what?*"

"Cottonreels and Missionaries and Sydney Views. And perhaps Triangular Capes."

"Never heard of them."

"Ah," said Appleby; "then you are one of those who have diamonds."

Poulish spooned up toheroa soup. "You don't seem to me to be the kind of man who gives himself away—unless accidentally on purpose."

Appleby shook his head. "I suddenly saw battle where I had thought there was only boredom. It made me incautious. But, as I was saying, you are living on diamonds while some of the others are living on stamps. I'm living on credit myself, which is one better still."

Involuntarily and somewhat uncertainly, Poulish smiled. "I could give you a tip or two on that . . . but, as you say, it's diamonds for me now. Lucky diamonds, as the phrase is. Things went to pieces while I was in quod, and it was—as your friend Mrs. Kittery says—a lucky break when diamonds came along."

"But the manner of their coming had its inconveniences? It meant, for instance, a discreet retreat?" Appleby looked placidly at his plate. A somewhat commonplace concoction of smoked oysters, he saw, had been substituted for the promised edible worms. "The situation was more or less that?"

"I am not concerned to contradict you." Poulish smiled with more confidence this time; it struck Appleby that the man had taken a liking to him.

"Quite so. And, in fact Sir Mervyn, it was because of the diamonds—and, of course, what you heard on the radio—that you murdered Unumunu?"

Poulish put down his fork, opened his eyes wide, turned slowly pale.

"May I ask," he said carefully, "what makes you put such an extraordinary question?"

"Haste. And may I ask you to answer it?"

"I will. I have never murdered anybody. Such a thing is not in my nature. I am a financier—a very dishonest one, as you know. When cornered we sometimes commit suicide. But homicide never. It is a matter of psychological type." And Poulish raised a glass to his lips with a slightly trembling hand.

There was a constrained silence. Looking up, Appleby saw Hoppo bobbing at him merrily from across the room; Miss Busst was having a success. Nearer at hand, Glover and Jenner were arguing vigorously. And, in a far corner, Miss Curricle was talking steadily and instructively to

Mr. Rumsby. He looked at Poulish again.

"I think you know Kimberley?"

It was some sort of hit. For the man blinked. "Yes . . . yes, of course I do."

"Well, you killed this Unumunu because you had heard over the radio that he knew too much about something at Kimberley. I suppose you got a glimpse of us when we were cast on the island, and recognized him. A horrid shock—and an astounding coincidence."

Poulish leant forward on his chair; he was pale to the lips now. "It's a fiendish lie!"

Appleby sighed. "You see that fellow Jenner over there? It's said that he kicked George."

"And what the devil of that?"

"Only that it's a fiendish lie too."

Coffee was on the veranda. Appleby, slipping to a solitary corner of this, presently found Diana beside him.

"Hullo," he said, "did you have a good dinner?"

"I had an old man who wasn't nice." Diana was brief. "What about you?"

"I've made a pal. And now I'm looking for more. What about trying Heaven? I think I can hear him coming."

There was a murmuring below them and presently they could see a dim round shape drifting through the darkness —rather like one of those aberrant and supernumerary moons which alarmed the Romans at the time of Caesar's murder. It mounted a flight of steps, and now was like a turnip-lantern on the end of a pole. Heaven, in a dinner-jacket and a billowing black tie, was coming to make the round of his guests. A clever chap, Appleby thought. He and his wife contrived to run something like a luxury hotel with the help of a pack of semi-savages. Which meant hard work, too. . . . "Good evening," he said.

Heaven stopped, smiled and bowed—to the accompaniment of those faint noises which suggested, somewhere about him, the presence of an invisible herd of elfin cattle.

"Good evening, sir; good evening, my dear madam. I hope our little effort at diversion was a success? *Dulce est desipere in loco*: we follow the Horatian rule."

"I should have thought not so much *in loco*," said Appleby, "as *in secula seculorum*. The non-stop Good Time, or what used to be called the Earthly Paradise. Your effort, Mr. Heaven, is at that. And I admire your temerity. It has been achieved in paint—Watteau did it and Giorgione too, though with Giorgione disturbing ideas crept in. But in actuality it has always broken down. In fact, *dis aliter visum* has been the memorial of all such schemes yet."

Diana sat down, saucer-eyed at this coruscation of culture. And Heaven rather uneasily laughed.

"The gods had other ideas? But we have other ideas about the gods. The Hermitage doesn't believe in them,

I am sorry to say."

"Are you sure? You think there is only one effective belief here, your own belief in money. But there may be people who worship other gods—and with surprising fervour. You belong to a past century, Mr. Heaven."

Heaven looked puzzled. "Really, I'm not sure of what you mean." He gave a chuckle and an inarticulate murmur. "Or whether you're being at all kind."

"Only kindness is intended. And what I mean is this. Your hotel, pitched at great cost and labour at the other end of nowhere to meet a foreseen demand, is an example of what used to be called Free Enterpise at its most enterprising. You rate profit so high that you are prepared to go a great distance for it. Perhaps you are prepared to go to great lengths too. Anyway it interests me. You must be a man of quite exceptional cupidity and greed."

"John," Diana interrupted mildly, "is this what you call making pals?"

"No; it's what I call making things clear. Mr. Heaven thinks he is the only person here with a drive—and his drive is towards money. Hence an Earthly Paradise reared on smuggled diamonds and stamps. If he sees any drive at all in other people it will be his own drive that he tends to see. But I am saying that there are other drives: more today than there were, say, fifty years ago. And he may fail to see them, largely because he is that old-fashioned thing, a materialist wrapped up as an aesthete.

He may fail to see them, when such a failure is dangerous."

"Really," said Heaven, "it is a great pleasure to meet so fresh and charming a mind. Particularly"—he turned and bowed to Diana—"when it is partnered by so fresh and—"

"I do advise you," Appleby cut in on the compliment, "to think it over."

"Be assured I shall." Heaven laughed and murmured. But he was nervous now; his body was swaying with its odd, butting motion; his hands were playing indecisively before his chest.

"And before it is too late."

Heaven made a new sound—something like a sharp hiss.

"What do you mean? What is this about other drives, and danger?"

"Other drives? I was saying that there are people who are out for other things than cash. Think of the scientists. Think, for example, of Hailstone and Dunchue over there, absorbed in their archaeology."

"To be sure." The man had recovered himself, and his next chuckle was genuine. "How easy it is to find convincing examples when one's basic position is sound. I shall no doubt be a convincing example myself one day of this futile endeavour to build a paradise beneath the moon —or some golden hours amid an age of lead."

"Ah," said Appleby, "you're coming nearer to it now. The man who sought gold and found lead. Put it something like that."

Colonel Glover and the person called Jenner were still arguing; they had come into view together on the veranda just as Heaven slipped away. Perhaps Glover was doing most of the talking, and certainly as they came up Jenner could be seen glancing with some anxiety at his watch. Diana nudged Appleby.

"John, if you want another learned and friendly chat here's a suitable victim."

"No. What I want this time is to find out whether I've been unmasked."

"I don't understand you a bit. Your intentions were much more—more lucid earlier on."

Appleby chuckled irreverently. "That was in our days of *dolce far niente*."

"And this time, I suppose, you'll put the important bits into Greek."

"That is one possibility."

Diana tossed her head. "What *do* you mean?"

"Well, I think Heaven is nosing after something in which he fancies the important bits are in Spanish. And perhaps *we*— Ah, Colonel, good evening. Mrs. Kittery and I are arguing about the dog."

"Dog? Well, there's a great deal of good arguing in dogs. Eh, Jenner? Opinions differ, you know. Spaniels now . . . often difficult to find common ground." Glover shook a dubious head.

"Very true, Colonel." Jenner was an ill-looking person who spoke with unexpected breeding and precision. "Not that I am a dog man, I am afraid." He turned politely to Diana. "Are you?"

"No, I'm not a dog man either. I mean, not a—" Caught by some interesting linguistic possibility, Diana disconcertingly laughed. "But we *weren't*—"

"We were speaking," said Appleby, "of the dog called George. Mrs. Kittery is not agreed that he is a nice dog." He turned to Jenner. "What do you think?"

"George? I kicked him." Again Jenner looked at his watch—this time with the frankest anxiety. "I think, if you will excuse me—" He bowed and vanished.

Appleby sighed gently. "Diana, what was that, Spanish or Greek?"

Diana shook her head glumly. "I think you must be going dippy."

"A sort of bald and unimaginative efficiency; where would you attribute that as a national characteristic?"

Diana was silent. Glover, who had been staring after Jenner, turned to Appleby. "As a national characteristic? Why, I should say—"

"Exactly."

17

It was characteristic of the Hermitage guests that they were subject at times to a species of endemic gloom. The trouble was that a Good Time is not really possible; all that can be achieved by the most determined pursuit is a series of Good Times with gaps in between; and on the island these gaps—should one fail to skip them successfully—were apt to widen into yawning crevasses of boredom or nervous unease.

Something of the sort, Appleby thought as he returned to the lounge, must have happened now. There was an indefinable tension in the air. The Younger Crush were looking dispirited—indeed, almost squashed; among the older people there was a tendency to abstraction—and subsequent recrimination—as they sat over their cards. Mr. Hoppo was still in attendance upon Miss Busst, but whereas at dinner he had appeared cheerful he was now unmistakably glum. Appleby went over and sat down between them.

"I've been outside," he said. "A pleasant night with a wisp of moon coming up."

"A new moon?" asked Miss Busst, and began to rummage in a little embroidered bag. "I can never tell."

Hoppo roused himself from an unwontedly reflective state. "Fair moon," he said, "we place no faith in you, because your tales are never true; you are not crescent when a C, nor yet declining when a D." He giggled half-heartedly. "A useful rhyme. But will it be the same in the southern hemisphere? I really don't know."

"Well," said Miss Busst, "just *in case*—" And she turned over some money in her bag. "It's stupid, of course, and I don't really believe in anything of that sort. But somehow tonight— I wonder who heard of it first?"

Appleby looked up idly. "Heard of it? There is some bad news?"

Miss Busst nodded solemnly. Hoppo cleared his throat.

"Of course," he said huskily, "it may be a false alarm. Apparently there has never been any suggestion of the sort before. But they say—*somebody* says . . . well, the savages."

"Ah," murmured Appleby, "the savages."

"I consider it very careless of the Heavens," said Miss Busst with sudden plain anger, "—very careless indeed. There was no mention of anything of the sort in the prospectus. It is perfectly scandalous. Of course there was a sort of Hawaiian girl on the cover—dressed in grasses, and that sort of thing. But it was understood that the intention was merely to catch the eye of possible guests, male guests. That there really were disagreeable natives anywhere near was never hinted at. No one thought that the island would be inconveniently placed in that way. I think the Heavens should be compelled to move."

"But are they near?" asked Appleby. "One doesn't seem to be able to get any accurate geographical information at all."

Hoppo glanced uneasily about the room. "They say— they say that *somebody* says—that there is an island with very unpleasant people about a hundred miles off. And then half-way to here there is a fishing-ground. They go there in *big* canoes. And if that isn't a success, if—well, if they fail to get provisions that way, then sometimes they go farther afield. That explains our own adventure. And now there is a rumour—"

"Ah," said Appleby again.

"A great many guests," said Miss Busst, "agree that the Heavens should be compelled to move the hotel. Mr. Rumsby is going to speak about it. With this dreadful war one's nerves are not in a state to be played upon in that way."

Appleby nodded. "I can see the possibility of a move having great advantages. Only I suspect that it is too late. You see, if the Heavens were going to move they would have to be capable of moving. But I see Miss Curricle beckoning. Will you excuse me?"

He crossed the room. Miss Curricle, exceedingly upright and angular, led him out once more to a veranda. "Mr. Appleby, there is every sign of a panic." She spoke with all of the hotel's sudden and pervading gloom—but at the same time with a certain dark satisfaction, as some literary satanist might speak of a horrid creation of his own. "It is exceedingly disgraceful and disagreeable. With the people at the bungalow we must muster a dozen able-bodied men. And surely somewhere there are fire-arms. Yet, at a rumour of those cowardly savages—"

"About the rumour—have you any idea where it started? It has sprung up uncommonly quick." Appleby was staring into the darkness as he spoke.

"Nobody seems to know. And the Heavens cannot be found. . . . Listen."

Appleby shook his head. "No good listening. Half the life on an island like this is nocturnal, and if one really listens one hears enough to make one's blood freeze. Which is scarcely what is wanted."

"I really thought I heard something like wary move-ment on the edge of the clearing."

"It is very likely. We are probably going to witness some rather terrible events. But I believe that there is, at present, no general danger. It depends, I am afraid, on whether, not so long ago, I sailed rather close to the wind."

"Mr. Appleby, you speak strangely. Perhaps I ought to say that I have confidence in you." Miss Curricle spoke with a faintly embarrassed briskness. "I am aware that when I was—ah—seeing matters in a somewhat faulty perspective during our adventures you behaved in a very level-headed way. Your manner is somewhat mysterious, but that is professional habit, no doubt. My dear father, who held a post of much responsibility in the civil service, carried discretion almost to a fault." Miss Curricle paused decently on this. She might be hearing alarming noises in the darkness, but she was not going to hurry over one of these periodical tributes. "I must say that I have become aware—and the others of our party agree with me—that there is something strange about the way of things here on the island. It is clear that you share this view. I wonder if you could tell me what you know? Incidentally"—Miss Curricle's voice was perfectly level—"I have just seen a naked figure near Mudge's hut. As it happens, I have a good eye in the dark. My dear mother had the same faculty. . . . But nothing, of course, which you think it desirable to keep to yourself."

"I can't tell you much." Appleby was looking at the little glow of light in Mr. Heaven's power-house. "For one thing I am very much in the dark—a dark I ought to have an eye like yours for—still, at the moment the dark." He paused. "But I know or suspect something, and a little time ago I was afraid I had given it away. Now I believe there is a good chance I didn't. The indiscretion is making me very close now. But I can tell you this. Heaven is a somewhat disreputable person, who sees all human activity in terms of grab. And this led him to suspect that Hailstone and Dunchue over there were not after what they professed. . . . You were right, by the way. I can see a couple of lurking figures myself. And here is Hoppo. Hoppo, go in and bring Glover and Mrs.

Kittery here; we'll stay together." Appleby looked absently for a moment after the surprised and retreating clergyman. Then he went on. "Heaven was so convinced that those first explorers of the island were frauds that he did a little quiet burglary."

"I am not surprised." Miss Curricle was tart. "No doubt we owe a certain gratitude for the sanctuary we have found, but I must say that I disapprove of this hotel very strongly. There is a man creeping round the corner of the veranda. Very strongly indeed."

"Heaven burgled Hailstone"—Appleby was now speaking to the little group of his companions—"and found something. Or so I conjecture. But this, by the way, is absolutely confidential. You understand me? Our lives may depend on it—and more than our lives."

Hoppo coughed. "This is most dramatic and startling. One should really feel uncommonly alarmed. But I believe one grows accustomed to fantastic dangers. I confess that at the moment curiosity is my chief emotion. As you know, I am not a courageous person. I am quite surprised."

"My dear fellow"—Glover spoke gruffly—"we have great confidence in you. And now let Appleby go on. Heaven burgled something. Now, burgled what . . . ? Good gad, there's a nigger with one of those spears."

"Let him alone. And just what Heaven burgled I can't tell. But I imagine it may have been an old Spanish chart —something like that. And that marked on it is a spot where you may dig up any amount of doubloons and pieces of eight."

"The wagon!" exclaimed Diana.

"Quite so: the barrow. Heaven found this chart, and during a curious little picnic this morning he deliberately revealed the fact to our archaeological friends—which was a great mistake. That is all that I can tell you at the moment—and more, I repeat, than you must tell anyone else. The sequel is going to be violent. . . . Ah!"

From across the clearing before them there had come a crash of splintered glass, and seconds later the little light vanished from the power-house. They swung round where they stood. The hotel was in darkness too.

"I suggest," said Appleby, "staying where we are. If we move we shall be encouraged to keep on moving—which would be rather a waste of physical effort on this debilitating island." There was a sudden scream from within the hotel. "I think that is Miss Busst faced with another Good Time. Presumably a frightful savage has climbed through her window. And there"—momentarily he flashed a torch on a bellowing figure bounding across the veranda and down a flight of steps—"there is Rumsby. Perhaps he has gone to fetch the police. Steady, now"— he raised his voice against a sudden pandemonium of howl- ing voices and beating drums all about them—"and re- member we have had all this before. It is possible that they will burn down the hotel, but on the whole I think not. . . . Look out."

There was a sound of rending wood and splintering

glass behind them as the frame of a window gave way from within. A figure tumbled through, picked itself up and ran—a brown and naked figure; it was followed by Sir Mervyn Poulish brandishing what appeared to be the leg of a chair. And Appleby laughed aloud above the tumult. "My heart warms towards that profoundly dishonest man." He checked himself. "Tomfoolery. But with tragedy at the core of it, I am sorry to say."

18

Dawn came luridly to the island, as if Sin and Death had thrown back their doors and admitted some reflection of the eternal bonfire to the sky. At least the elements were preparing a demonstration—and Miss Busst, not without hints of the hand of Providence, thought it likely that the retreating savages would be scattered about the deeps. For over what had happened Miss Busst was bitterest of all. She had been assaulted by a gigantic native; he had pranced round her howling, that was to say, and before making off had seemed almost disposed to tweak her nose. Mr. Heaven would abundantly have heard about it if Mr. Heaven had not been dead.

The finding of the body was announced by Dunchue, who explained that its discovery was the first intimation of the raid that the bungalow had received. For he and Hailstone had gone off camping for the night—each admitted to a faint interest in nocturnal turtle-hunting—and it was as they returned that some excitement on the part of George led to the discovery of the dead man among the sand-hills. Whereupon they had left one of their boys on guard and hurried to the hotel. Dunchue, having less leisure in his soul, arrived considerably in advance.

He found an Appleby who was doing his best hastily to fortify the place against a second night raid. Windows were being barricaded and buckets of sand and water prepared against any attempt to employ fire. It would be useless, Appleby explained, against an enemy armed with any species of guns. But against these noisy but not very courageous natives it might do. Mudge was preparing some harmless—but it was hoped frightening—grenades.

Dunchue listened to a recital of these preparations with what, had he known it, Appleby analysed as a mixture of malice and genuine satisfaction. And he gave his bad news reluctantly. There it was. These noisy intruders had made their second kill. If somebody from the hotel would come along and have a look they could then arrange for bearers to bring the body in. Perhaps Appleby himself would come. At this Appleby scratched his chin and suggested that quite a number of people should go.

Things had progressed so far when a blob of variegated colour on the beach heralded the arrival of the more ponderous Hailstone and the attendant George. Both were decently subdued. One almost expected the gay umbrella to have trimmings in black *crêpe*.

"A shocking thing," said Hailstone. "We sympathize with you all." He patted George. "But, of course, with Mrs. Heaven first of all. I think I should go to her at once. George, come."

It was explained that Mrs. Heaven had disappeared. When this had been discovered just before dawn, Jenner, with considerable gallantry, had ventured all round the environs of the hotel in search of her; with Mudge and Colonel Glover he was out on a wider sweep now. Hailstone looked anxious.

"A woman!" he said; "this is more terrible still."

Miss Busst offered an inarticulate noise; several female guests began to weep; Mr. Rumsby, who had unprecedentedly got his own breakfast, called out urgently to know if anyone were preparing luncheon. And then a party was arranged to go and inspect the late proprietor of the hotel. Dunchue had a shot-gun and remained to guard the majority of the agitated guests. Hailstone had an ancient and ineffective looking revolver; this he offered to Appleby, who courteously declined to relieve him of it. The two set off together with a little crowd behind them.

For once Hailstone contrived to combine pedestrianism and conversation.

"I am afraid," he said, "that we must both cry *peccavi*. I confess that over your black friend Unumunu I was sceptical; it did not appear to me that any natives in these parts were likely to commit such an act. And I think you were sceptical too. But now—well, the thing seems beyond argument."

The blue glasses turned sharply on Appleby. And Appleby replied with faint reluctance, "Yes, there can be no doubt of it."

"I tell you frankly that I think there is no hope for

that wretched woman. A first crime was a surprise, and I think that only his being a black man brought it about. But a kill quickly influences these Polynesian people for the worse; if they taste blood in a place once they will go for it there again."

Appleby nodded. "You speak," he said ingenuously, "as if you had some interest in the local anthropology after all."

Hailstone laughed a still decently muted laugh. "Nothing but a little casual reading. Dunchue knows more than I do, and he knows little enough. Enough, perhaps, to strike up some sort of possible relations with these invaders—nothing more."

"Ah," said Appleby.

"Here is Heaven dead and his wife no doubt dead or next to dead too. You and I will not waste sympathy on them. Their trade with these skulkers and escapists was scarcely a noble one. What we must consider is the practical problem."

"Exactly. In fact I have been considering it for some time."

Again Hailstone glanced quickly at his companion. But Appleby's eye was mildly on the dignified forward wobble of George. "All these people will almost certainly want to leave, and one can scarcely blame them. They have nothing to tie them to the island."

"Unlike yourself, Mr. Hailstone."

"Quite so. We couldn't, of course, leave the dig, and

we must take our chance. It is a thousand pities that the wireless is out of order. Have you any skill with such things?"

"None at all, I am afraid."

"A pity again. It really seems necessary to call for help. Fortunately Dunchue has reminded me of something I had forgotten. Our trader is not positively engaged to look in on us for some months. But now we remember that the skipper said something which makes it possible that it will be back quite soon. And it could take everybody away."

"Well, nothing could be better than that."

"Quite so." Again Appleby was aware of a swift scrutiny. "Only there is one thing that troubles me, and with your acuteness you will at once guess what it is."

Appleby shook his head. "I find any guessing peculiarly difficult here, no doubt because the environment is wholly strange to me. I must confess that my only thought at present is to get back to London and my own job."

Hailstone nodded approvingly. "You will know that I sympathize. To be away from one's work is wretched."

They walked for a few moments in silence, as if digesting these improving sentiments.

"But at a venture," continued Appleby, "I should say that, with the interest of the dig in mind, you don't want any sort of fuss."

"Exactly," said Hailstone, and paused for a breather. George, pausing too, wagged his tail. Things were going with a wonderful unanimity. "Exactly. But it cannot be denied that from an official point of view something very serious has occurred. And when our friends start spreading it about—"

"I think they will be discreet. After all, their position is rather delicate—ridiculous, indeed. They are pitched with their stamps and diamonds out of their earthly paradise and back into a jarring world. I don't think they'll talk."

"But," said Hailstone—and he resumed his walk— "there are your companions and yourself."

Appleby appeared to consider. "I believe that Colonel Glover and I could use a little influence which would ensure that the island should not be publicized. Of course we couldn't prevent an inquiry—at least I don't *think* we could—but we could see that it would not go beyond official circles. I think I can undertake that, even if the jurisdiction here should prove to be American. If you feel it would help, that is."

"My dear sir, I am exceedingly grateful. Perhaps we are discussing the matter prematurely. But you know how afraid I am of unwelcome notoriety."

"I do, indeed."

They walked on in silence. Appleby glanced at their two shortening shadows on the sand. Neither at all knowing where he had the other. Bluff? Double bluff? It was like a sort of peripatetic poker.

"The body is round this hummock," said Hailstone.

"One of my boys is with it, though I fear sadly scared. Ah! I hadn't thought the ants would be so quick."

Heaven's body sprawled on its face. A spear had been thrust through his back and still stuck there. All his clothes had been wrenched off and had vanished. As he had lain dying or dead there had been some ugly writhing at his neck and limbs. Now the ants were eating him. It was, in its comparatively simple way, a peculiarly horrible death.

Appleby looked at the body with a sort of mild attention, undisturbed by the exclamations of the men behind him. He turned to Hailstone.

"I wonder how they got him? I last saw him at the hotel not very long before the raid. We had a conversation—it seems oddly inappropriate now—about gold and lead. Dear, dear!"

"Gold and lead?" Hailstone was startled.

"A futile literary conversation," said Appleby easily. "He was, you know, by way of being aesthetically inclined. Yes, about the golden and leaden caskets in *The Merchant of Venice*. And now, what with all these ants, he could do with a leaden casket himself. Is Hoppo with us? Ah, yes. Well, I suggest that a quick burial will be the decent and least troublesome thing. Our efforts should be directed to making sure about his wife. They may have carried her off—perhaps only to some other part of the island. With at least a couple of fire-arms I think we might risk a search-party. Don't you think?" And Appleby, practical and level-headed, but neither very forceful nor very concerned, looked inquiringly at Hailstone.

"I think you are quite right." Hailstone nodded almost briskly. "It is a great comfort to have someone who always gets an accurate grasp of an affair." He turned and spoke to the waiting boy.

They buried Heaven. In half-an-hour he had vanished. The pace of things, Appleby thought, was improving . . . if it could be put that way. He walked down to the sea. Here within the reefs the waves were very small and lapping, they followed one another almost secretly to the shore. Fish darted—so tiny that they could loop and wheel in the utmost shallows; a crab, like some magically liberated shadow, scuttled from stone to sheltering stone. The tiny drag of the receding wavelets shifted the sands, raised and caught into its gyres a myriad all-but-ultimate particles of matter, lost itself in contrary or transverse impulses which carried on the ceaseless motion. It was like a reading in Bergson: change and again change, without anything that did the changing. Heaven, Hailstone and Heraclitus, Appleby said to himself—and looked up to see this world of continual flux declaring and intensifying itself on the beaches. He watched idly, his mind a thin trickle of philosophers' clichés, unaware of any practical significance in what he saw. The air was still about him but in the middle distance Hailstone's trousers, George's fleece were faintly stirring; a breeze more stealthy than the lapping, secret waves was scurrying over the sands, a slurring movement as swift and close-gliding as a furtive caress. And on the sands those strange fibrous balls with which Diana played had still been piling; they were there in thousands and millions now, as if all the Sirens had played at tip-and-run through all the ages and every hit had been out of bounds. And the low-creeping wind thrust at them with exploratory fingers, turned them over, rolled them one against another in an endless complication of cannons, tentatively tossed them a few inches in air. The smaller of the light, dun spheres began to hop on the beach—clumsily, like sand-lice or like tiddly-winks inexpertly flipped. And far down the beach something which Appleby had taken for a boulder stirred and fluttered, raised a sudden dark pennon which flapped in air. He shouted. And everyone was hurrying that way.

Mrs. Heaven's dark skirt, water-stained, lay on the sand; in a drained rock pool was a soggy shift; yards out on the almost calm but obscurely hurrying water a boot grotesquely floated. Hailstone lumbered up, pointed, exclaimed. In the sand close by was a great bold gash such as the blunt knife of a giant might have made. Appleby stared, momentarily puzzled. Hailstone turned to him.

"Canoe." He measured the gash with his eye. "A big one."

Appleby nodded. "It must be big if they think nothing of covering a hundred miles." He looked up at the sky, where a hue of copper was spreading out mysteriously from the zenith. "Poor lady; she's going to have a rough voyage, too. A pity she couldn't have had Miss Busst to keep her company." He looked out to sea, decently troubled. "The sooner your trader arrives the better. And it rather complicates things, does it not, if she has been carried away alive. We can't just try to hush up the whole thing. She must be hunted for."

Hailstone nodded—a shade reluctantly, as if this aspect of the matter had not struck him.

"Of course." He looked at his watch. "Would it be any use asking you back to lunch?"

"I think not; I must try to get things better organized at the hotel. But this afternoon—and if this coming storm doesn't prevent me—I shall stroll over." Appleby paused —paused until Hailstone's eye was drawn to him. Then he smiled a deliberately enigmatic smile. "Because you and I must have another little talk."

"By all means." The man was startled.

"They won't keep her alive long, I imagine. Livestock for the voyage, as likely as not."

Hailstone nodded, looking slightly shocked.

"So why, after all, make a fuss? I think we can arrange something together." And Appleby gave a little grin— as vicious as he could manage—and turned back towards the hotel.

19

COLONEL GLOVER PUT DOWN HIS GLASS OF LEMON WATER. "How did you begin to suspect the truth?"

Appleby and his companions, together with Sir Mervyn Poulish, were eating a scrap luncheon on a corner of the veranda. Mudge was waiting on them. And from within came the agitated and querulous voices of the other guests.

"The truth? I haven't arrived there yet." Appleby smiled grimly. "And we may all be dead—and in the tummies of Dunchue's imaginary cannibals—before I do."

Mr. Hoppo took a very deliberate bite at a sandwich. He munched. "Dunchue?" he said. "Dunchue rather than Hailstone?"

"Decidedly. Dunchue is the leader. Hailstone, you know, is a Eurasian, and Dunchue regards him as of an inferior race. He told him so more or less to my face. They're a good team, but that they love each other I wouldn't be prepared to say."

Glover was looking doubtful. "A Eurasian? I can hardly believe—"

"He never takes those blue glasses off. Once he began to do so when Diana and I were at the bungalow, but when he saw us he just took off his panama instead. But he *did* take them off right at the beginning and to get a good look at me on the beach. I was puzzled at once. There was a sort of betwixt-and-betweenness about him, if you know what I mean. And then I rifled his desk and found an opium pipe and what was almost certainly a tin of opium. That settled it. He must have lived in England for years, but a Eurasian he is. That, however, is a detail. I got on the right trail when we first met, and in the simplest way. It has been among my chief anxieties to reflect that he must have reckoned on my doing so. You see, on an island in the middle of nowhere an anthropologist is murdered, and the next thing that happens is that a fellow of the same or kindred species turns up. It is an amazing coincidence, and perhaps our bungalow friends showed a poor judgment in trying, with their savages and whatnot, to carry it off."

Miss Curricle turned a faintly disapproving eye from Diana's coco-cola to Appleby. "Now that you make the point—"

"Exactly. It often takes a professional to realize the force of a coincidence. Well, what was the real connection between those scientists—Hailstone and Dunchue on the one hand and Unumunu on the other? It could hardly be one of close anterior association; after all, we had been cast up on this island absolutely at random. But a Negro anthropologist must be something of a rarity, and they may have known him and recognized him. Or—more likely, this, because our friends may not be archaeologists at all—they met him on the morning of his death and among his explanations was some account of his profession. Whereupon he died. Why? Presumably because they at once feared that he would show them up. Their activities were not such as to stand the scrutiny of a mind trained in the branch of science they professed. I had that as the most likely run of the thing from the first."

Diana's eyes had rounded and grown far-away. Perhaps, by some association of ideas, she was contemplating once more a mental picture of Mr. Bradman at the crease.

"And to think, John, that you had all that in your head when we met Dunchue drunk in the jungle!"

"Drunk?" A fleeting smile lit the now curiously settled anxiety on Appleby's face. "My second discovery lay just there. He wasn't drunk. You remember our luncheon at the bungalow? He gave us each a drink—and at that drink I can now remember looking in a puzzled way. But at the time I didn't see the point until slightly later. It was after we had lunched and I was sitting looking out at a table on the veranda. A highly polished table. *And it was spotless*. Yet Dunchue, when absolutely tight to all appearance, had set me down a brimming drink on it. You see? It was a bad slip and his drunkenness was revealed as a pretence. I was confirmed in the knowledge that the bungalow was a fake. But how much of a fake?"

"Ah," said Poulish, "that's often the problem. Believe me."

"They had killed Unumunu simply to prevent his discovering something. Could it be simply what they then so quickly admitted to Diana and me—that their find was not a matter of Pacific archaeology proper, but of Viking explorers? I thought not. It was more likely that their fear was that they would be discovered as concerned with something which could not rightly be classed as scientific archaeology at all. And this was the conclusion to which our friend Heaven came too. There was a point at which, in an irresponsible mood which I now bitterly regret, I almost gave myself away. But Heaven gave himself away deliberately, and as a preliminary, as he thought, to coming to terms with them. In that he sadly failed to take their measure. Their reply was to fudge up another raid by those savages they had first invented to cover Unumunu's death. The Heavens were eliminated and the whole hotel given good reason to want to quit. If possible, they want that quitting to be so arranged that there will be no inquiries either by government or connections of the Heavens or anyone else. I think that is why we have not been wiped out; a wipe-out would bring exhaustive investigations once Heaven's yacht, say, came in. They hope to eliminate the hotel now with virtually no questions asked. It is very difficult. They have to think it out. And in that lies our chance."

Mudge had been clearing dishes from the table. He paused in this. "It does suggest, Mr. Appleby, that a man may smile and smile and be a villain. It's wonderful, in a manner of speaking, how life has the trick of vindicating art." He was silent for a moment on this meditative note. "A very pleasant-spoken person that Mr. Hailstone seemed to me to be. And I almost hesitate, sir, to believe in such desperate villainy. And I'm sure Sir Mervyn agrees with me."

"I do agree with Mudge." Poulish placidly sipped whisky. "The psychology of those people doesn't seem to me to be coming out right. A wipe-out? No, I don't somehow recognize it among my acquaintance. Which has been pretty extensive in the last few years, I may say."

Appleby nodded gravely. "The picture is still very imperfect. And I must say that I am afraid our danger is increasing. I believe that as things stand at the moment Dunchue and Hailstone will only have to reflect a little to see an extreme danger in letting us away at all. Trained minds—and one that of a professional detective officer"—he shook his head—"it makes me dislike the sound of their trader which they say may be in soon." He looked round their anxious and still slightly bewildered faces. "However, I have a last trick to play, and I play it this afternoon."

There was a silence, and then Hoppo spoke. "The cannibals: you are quite sure—?"

"Quite. Our friends, plus their own native boys, plus one or two people whom you can guess at nearer home."

"In fact"—Hoppo's voice betrayed an uncertain movement between relief and regret—"we are not up against savages at all; only some sort of white criminals?"

"That, more or less." Appleby paused, serious and absorbed. "Not criminals, though."

They stared at him. "But," said Diana, "Ponto—"

"Mrs. Heaven—" said Miss Curricle.

Appleby shook his head. "It's a very difficult question. You see—"

He was interrupted by a startling scream from close at hand. It was followed by another and another, so that people hurried from the hotel to look. And suddenly from the undergrowth before them broke the running figure of Miss Busst, her arms waving in imbecile terror before her.

"The savages," she screamed; "the savages have killed another man!"

The body was naked—that of a middle-aged man, clean-shaven, with two great gashes as of sabre-cuts across the cheeks. Of the little group which had set out to find it at Miss Busst's directions Jenner was the first to speak.

"An absolute stranger. Well, I'll be damned!"

Appleby looked at Jenner and wondered. Then he looked at the mysterious body as it lay in a little clearing. And finally he looked at the sky. In a way the sky was more interesting than anything else; with dead bodies he was familiar enough, but he had never seen such a sky as this. It was the colour of old bronze, in places smeared with dull green like a patina; it was as if the elements were constructing some disproportionate mausoleum for this, the island's latest enigma. But it was, too, as if with this vast canopy nature's interest in the mystery had ceased; the birds offered no threnody; there was no whispered question in the grasses. Everything had gone profoundly still. The little creeping wind had faded. One could feel that even the tiniest living things had stowed themselves away and that the dead man had been lying in a loneliness unusual even here.

Glover was looking with an old eastern campaigner's dispassionateness at the wounds.

"Wanton," he said. "Nasty ritual trick, no doubt." He seemed suddenly puzzled. "Look here, Appleby, if what you say is true—"

"Yes," said Appleby loudly, "if I'm right we're far from out of the wood yet." He turned to Jenner. "I was telling the Colonel I associate this with the new moon. Time of some big feast, probably, and they need victims. I suspect the brutes mean to come back for this chap to-night." During these remarks he shot Glover a look that was far from flattering. "Question is, how did the fellow —a white man—get here? It's impossible he can have been living on the island. Can you think of any explanation, Mr. Jenner?"

Jenner shook a head in which the eyes, oddly, stayed steadily on Appleby. "I don't know that I can."

"Well, I have an idea." Appleby paused a little, as if he wished no one to miss a display of professional acuteness.

"Rather a horrid one, too. I think they probably captured him some time back and have been carrying him round. Till the ritual moment came, you know. Poor devil." He stared rather callously—a shade owlishly even—at the corpse. "Best shove him under. At it all day." He laughed sharply. "And then look out for ourselves. Strengthen those barricades." He paced restlessly up and down. "I wish that damned trader would come. We have Dian— women to think of, after all." He looked up suddenly, suspiciously at the little circle of men. "That's right, isn't it?" Again he strode up and down, a man not in any too good command of his nerves. "Hailstone and Dunchue are determined to stay. The more fools they. Unless"— the words seemed to slip out—"they feel on better terms with the brutes than I do." He broke off abruptly, angrily. "Glover, Hoppo—for God's sake go and get a couple of spades. And never mind if you forget that prayer-book. Lord knows what sort of a storm we're in for with a sky like that above us." He looked down at the body, and his laugh was now both sharp and coarse. "Didn't even leave the poor bastard his pants."

The stranger was being buried—not thanks to any assistance of Appleby's, for Appleby had disappeared. He might have been found in the semi-darkness of the late Mr. Heaven's closed boat-house, anxiously watching a tinkering Mudge.

"I thought they might," he said. "They're thorough.

And I'm trying to be thorough too. . . . Is it bad?"

"I think not, Mr. Appleby. They've thought it best not to do anything too obvious, it seems. Covert guile, sir. Did you ever read Dr. Erasmus Darwin's *Economy of Vegetation?*"

Appleby stared. "What the devil has that to do with it?"

Mudge looked surprised. "Nothing at all, to be sure, sir. Just a passing of the time."

"Oh, I see. I beg your pardon. No, I'm afraid I never have."

"I think I could recommend *The Loves of the Plants.* Not reflective, exactly; but very pretty in its way. It's the magneto, I'm glad to say, sir. I have a spare one boxed up there in the corner. If they'd removed the plugs, now, it would be a different thing. And instructive, Mr. Appleby. It takes a full mind to write poetry on botanical subjects. Would you just lift those boards at your feet, now, and see what you can see? You'll find they're loose, though they don't look it."

Appleby did as he was told. "I see a couple of tins of petrol."

"Well now, that's something." In the half-light Mudge grinned solemnly. "You never know. That's what I said to myself when I stowed it away. Only I wish now, sir, I'd stowed away a little more of it."

"But surely you have plenty elsewhere?"

"Yes, Mr. Appleby. Enough for quite a voyage. But covert guile again, sir. The drums seem tight enough. But just flash your torch on the floor about them and see what you can see."

Again Appleby obeyed. "A few white grains of something."

"Of course there are critics, Mr. Appleby, who would maintain that Dr. Darwin's verse has a saccharine quality, so to speak. Sugary, sir. By the way, just put one of those grains on your tongue." Mudge grinned again. "Yes, Mr. Appleby: sugar. A little sugar goes a long way with petrol. Covert guile, sir."

20

THE SKY HAD DARKENED FURTHER WHEN APPLEBY LEFT the boat-house; to look up was to feel oneself within some vast bubble of congealed blood. On the ocean no flurry of wind, no trace even of swell was perceptible—but mysteriously nevertheless the breakers still crashed on the reef and tossed their white manes high in the pervading breathlessness, like asphyxiated creatures rearing desperately to gulp at air. The island waited. It was curious that nature should be concerned to build up such portentous threats instead of getting on with whatever release of forces was proposed. Appleby went to find Diana.

"Will you come?" he asked gravely.

She looked at him, surprised. "To the bungalow? But of course."

"I wouldn't ask you—only you're a necessary part of the plan."

"Gallant to the last. For it is about the last, isn't it?"

"There is a good deal of risk blowing about."

Diana swung herself from the rail on which she was perched. "Then come on. It's nice to be necessary—a change from being desired." She threw mockery into the word, whistled a sickly tune, broke off. "No more gramophone; just bugles and trumpets. A minstrel boy to the war is gone." She stretched herself, looked down at her flexed knees, at the clear line of her shins. "Only I should hate to perish in Miss Busst's second-best shorts."

They set off past the swimming-pool. The water was black like velvet and with a glow as of submarine fire in the shadows. It might have been Grendel's mere or the haunt of some Viking dragon. A big rubber animal, half deflated, spun slowly at its centre. On the steps were cigarette ends, a bitten biscuit, a highly coloured cherry impaled on a little stick. The place was heavy with the prophecy of a Hermitage Hotel to let.

"Jenner's disappeared—and another man who's a bit of a pal of his." Diana spoke low in the clamant hush about them.

Appleby nodded. "They're concentrating their forces —just in case."

"John, what was that about Jenner kicking George? You know, you've made it a sort of favourite theme."

"Jenner didn't kick George. But Hailstone told me— somewhat gratuitously—that he did. It's my business to spot lies—to feel the tiny psychological discontinuities that mark a dive from the truth—and I spotted that one. But the spotting of it was almost my undoing. I imme-diately asked Hailstone whether Jenner had arrived with the second lot of guests. You see, I was excited and a bit careless. The issues hadn't come home to me then and I just showed off—a thing a policeman shouldn't do."

"Showed off?"

"My question revealed far too good an understanding of the affair. You must realize that the arrival of Heaven and his hotel was a bit of a blow to our friends. They wanted the island to themselves—as they do now. And if they couldn't get that, then they wanted to keep the balance of physical power on their own side. So they brought up reinforcements—quite cunningly as guests to the hotel. The reinforcements were Jenner and a couple of others whom I think I've got taped now. It was as an unnecessary move to dissimulate this connection that Hailstone suggested a particular unfriendliness in Jenner; he had kicked George. I ought to have kept my instinctive sense of the lie to myself. But instead I almost betrayed it by asking the logical question. Had this Jenner come with the second lot of guests? It gave Hailstone a jolt at the time, and I enjoyed that. But I think—unless his bluff is deeper than I imagine—that he has since dismissed it as coincidence. Not that it's of great importance any longer. Because what you and I are up to now is sailing in and saying we *know*—just you and me."

Diana stared at him. "It does seem as if you were right in saying that there was risk blowing about. Not that I'm not all for it. Only I think it a little unfair that I *don't* know."

"My dear, it's not that that's unfair. It's what I'm going to say about you."

"What are you going to say?"

"Truth and lies, and both equally unfair. You will be shocked and angry." Appleby was speaking very soberly. "But don't forget to back me up like hell."

"I'll back you up."

He glanced at her curiously. She was looking puzzled and still a little aggrieved. Her eyes had brightened. Perhaps she was breathing a shade fast.

"You feel all right about this?" he asked softly.

"I feel extra," she said.

The jungle was very still; there was not even the slither of a sleepy lizard and the winding path to the bungalow was as noiseless as if its overarching greenery were a giant alga on the floor of ocean. It was like moving through a trance, a dream, an island under an enchanter's spell. Appleby put out his hand and rustled a clump of grasses as he passed; the sound was loud and threatening, like rain on a tin roof.

"It's as if everything had died with the Heavens," he said.

"John, what about that strange man—the body?"

He laughed softly. "Diana, you didn't think Mrs. Heaven was a woman, did you? Not with that voice and beard and stride? He was just Heaven's business partner, and for running a hotel man-and-wife was the convenient thing. Perhaps he was the sort of nerve-case who has a hankering for women's clothes; I don't know. But Dunchue used the queer truth of the matter brilliantly to reinforce the notion of a raid. They stripped the poor fellow's body, shaved it, gashed it about the face—and there you are. Mrs. Heaven had been carried off and the body of a strange man left lying about. I took care to offer Jenner the explanation he would presently have advanced himself—the cannibals had been carrying a wretched captive round. . . . But the truth about Mrs. Heaven will be one of the things we don't know."

"I see. No use being brighter than need be."

"That's it."

They were near the bungalow. "George ought to meet us about here," Diana said. But there was no George— and they realized that his appearance would have been something friendly and vital in a scene so utterly drained of life. The tree-ferns stood around them like motionless inverted cascades. To their left was a momentary glimpse of beach—invisible beneath its myriads of those strange sea-apples which now were inert and dead once more. Brilliantly white against an arc of darkening sky a single sea-gull, startlingly mobile, dipped and wheeled. Then again the jungle was around them.

"It seems farther this time," Diana said.

"We're just there." He put his arm round her waist, tightened his grip as she looked at him in surprise. "We walk like this. And feel like it too."

She stopped. "John, what do you mean? Feel like what?"

He looked at her anxiously. "Not as we really do. Not pleased with each other and independent too. Rather messed up with one another—and not awfully trustfully. The loves of the octopuses. Think of that."

She shivered. "You do put things neatly. Alright."

"*All right.*"

They laughed low together and stepped out into the glade.

The little bed of English cottage flowers. The veranda blinds, trim and gay. And on the veranda Jenner. He stared at them and without turning his head called something back into the darkness behind him. Appleby dropped his hand reluctantly from Diana's side.

"Good afternoon," he called out. There was something like a ring of defiance in his voice.

Jenner said nothing at all. They mounted the veranda steps. Hailstone's voice came from the shadowy living-room beyond.

"Appleby? Come in—come in." They entered. And Jenner slipped in behind them and stood by the door.

Beethoven and archaeology; the room was unchanged. Dunchue was unchanged; he rose and bowed to Diana, fell back clumsily in his chair.

"Something filthy coming up," he said. "Filthy tropics. . . . Find a drink." He looked vague and lowering round.

Appleby glanced at Jenner, hesitated. "I didn't think you would be having other visitors this afternoon." He nodded Diana brusquely into a chair; sat down rather sulkily himself.

"Ah." Hailstone was making tea with a spirit kettle;

there was no sign of any of the native boys. "Well, as a matter of fact, we have been becoming rather friendly with Jenner just recently. We don't hide our plans from him."

Suddenly and harshly Appleby laughed. "Why pretend? Why pretend you kicked George—eh, Mr. Jenner?" He laughed again. "You see we know the whole thing—Mrs. Kittery and I, that is."

There was a moment's tense silence. Dunchue's right hand, as he slouched in his chair, crept to a pocket. Hailstone held the spirit kettle suspended.

"And we needn't quarrel." Appleby looked warily round him. "We've no desire to go the way the Heavens went—or that poor chap we found this morning. Did you set the savages on him too?"

Hailstone put down the kettle. "I don't understand you," he said quietly. "We are not responsible for any of those deaths."

"Aren't you?" Appleby looked momentarily uncertain of himself. "I suppose you deny that Heaven *knew?*"

There was another pause. Dunchue's hand came out of his pocket. The tension in the room just perceptibly slackened.

"Suppose Heaven did know something," asked Hailstone, "you don't think we'd take to murder, do you? The savages just happened."

"And I suppose they just happened to Unumunu too— Unumunu who would know you weren't going to dig out of that barrow anything at all like what you professed?" Appleby laughed again, the laugh of a knowing and unscrupulous man. "But I'm not here to talk about corpses."

Abruptly Dunchue sat up and was sober. "We understood you were a police officer. If you really believe we have been putting people out of the way—"

"I'd better explain." Appleby glanced quickly at Diana. "Things have changed for me since I came to the island. Mrs. Kittery here—Diana." He put up his chin arrogantly. "She's my mistress."

Dunchue raised his eyebrows. It was, Appleby noted with discomfort, a genuine gesture.

"I am sure we congratulate you both," he said suavely. And his eye went keenly to Diana. Diana looked sulky, put her toes together and smoothed her shorts with noticeable modesty. She had got the idea.

"And I'm going to marry her."

"To be sure." Dunchue, who had so recently signed the death warrant of several people, was faintly disdainful. "And are we to take it that at the same time she will marry you?"

"Of course." Appleby was obtuse, slightly angry. "Only there's Kittery. An ugly bastard, by all accounts. And he won't arrange to be divorced."

Hailstone poured out tea. "May I ask," he said mildly, "how you know that?"

Appleby looked at Diana. And Diana noisily sniffed.

"It was like that once before," she said—and looked slyly from Hailstone to Dunchue. "After all, it's natural, in a way."

"But we think he'll be willing to do the divorcing. So that's all right; we don't mind. Only it will be the end of me at the Yard."

"I won't be without anything," said Diana, suddenly practical and sharp. "I've told him that." And she contrived to look at her lover with a sort of infatuated mistrust.

"So you see"—Appleby appeared to find some difficulty in expressing himself—"we have to keep an eye to the main chance."

Hailstone handed tea. "I am sorry that George isn't here to witness this. It would extend his knowledge of human nature. But the pertinacious creature is still burrowing away at the dig. He puts us all to shame." He smiled at Appleby. "Don't you feel?"

Appleby scowled. "I don't give a curse for your dog. But your dig's another matter. It's time we got to that."

"It is, indeed. We ought to have got to it long ago." Dunchue was sipping tea. He was tall, upright, handsome, arrogant, with pale-blue Saxon eyes. "This island, as I have said before, has a bad effect on one. Character rapidly degenerates on it, Mr. Appleby." He smiled thinly beneath searching eyes.

It was fifty-fifty, Appleby thought, or perhaps less good than that. Hailstone, yes; he lacked a final knowledge of western man. But Dunchue had an informed critical intelligence which it would require something like inspiration to deceive. Better acknowledge oneself stung. . . . He sprang to his feet.

"Damn your superior airs, Mr. bloody-clever Dunchue! Do you think I take you for any better than the pirate-scum you're jackalling after? Talk business, or I'll know what to do." He turned to the door, where Jenner stood silent and immobile still.

"Don't be silly, John!" Diana had flashed into temper. "I tell you I won't have nothing. Sit down."

Appleby sat down. Dunchue looked at him impassively and in silence for some seconds.

"Well," he said at length, "what's your proposition?"

"I'll take five thousand pounds."

Dunchue turned to Hailstone, lazily smiled, said nothing.

"No less. I know you're after a big hidden treasure and are waiting to get at it quietly; that you were just getting at it when the hotel came. I know Heaven found out; stole the chart that told the story. I know he showed it to you under my nose, up there on top of the stuff." Appleby grinned cunningly. "And I know what happened to him. I know you can bring down a pack of murdering natives; I was a fool once to think myself too smart to believe in them. I believe in them now—and I've taken certain steps accordingly."

"Would it be too much to ask what they are?" Dunchue was looking thoughtful now.

"I don't think you'll care to risk a wholesale slaughter. And I've taken means you won't easily hit on to tell what I know when those people make some sort of civilization again. So it's no good Jenner standing by the door there with a gun in his pocket. He may as well sit down and take it easy."

Dunchue sighed, gave an almost imperceptible nod. And Jenner moved aside and sat down sullenly in a chair.

"Five thousand pounds. May I ask if we are to have anything but the uncertain prospect of your silence in return?"

"You can have a lot. Heaven's suckers won't talk; they'll be glad to go off and find another funk-hole quietly. And my lot won't talk by the time I've spun them a tale. You see"—and Appleby hesitated, seemed almost to flush—"they believe in me."

"Like Mrs. Kittery." Dunchue faintly smiled. "Anything else?"

"Yes. I can contact Heaven's yacht quick and settle with it. I can do the same with any creditors or relations. If nobody loses money they won't particularly bother in times like these about a couple of folk who came to a queer end while running a queer racket. You can have that. And I say five thousand pounds."

"Really"—Dunchue turned to Hailstone—"it seems a very attractive proposition. Will it occur to him, I wonder, that in proportion to the probable value of the treasure he's asking absurdly little?"

"Down," said Appleby quickly. "I said five thousand down. And a share out later."

Dunchue laughed with sudden convinced good humour. "I really believe we understand each other, Mr. Appleby. As you know, with all my airs I'm nothing but a low-down crook; and it's plain that you're another. Begging Mrs. Kittery's pardon."

Jenner, who was sitting staring out of the window, suddenly muttered something which Appleby didn't catch. Both Dunchue and Hailstone hurried over to join him. And Diana breathed in Appleby's ear, "John, are we winning?"

He nodded briefly. "So far. And if nothing out of the way—"

His words were drowned by a sudden shattering roar, as indescribable as the opening up of a heavy barrage. The three men had run out to the veranda and they followed. About them, everything was still perfectly still; there was no flutter in the veranda blinds, the gay little bed of flowers might have been painted on silk. It was only far over the sand-hills that some gigantic and concentrated disturbance had broken out. They stared unbelievingly. For in the sky was a great pillar of sand.

"A willy-willy!" Diana was shouting in Appleby's ear. "And it must be just over—"

"It's over the—" Dunchue's voice, raised high above the uproar, broke off abruptly.

And then there came another and inexplicable sound. If some giant child had tied a string of tin cans to the tail of a dragon just such a clatter might have been the result. The noise grew, faded, ceased. The pillar of sand—the great vortex of sand—began to move slowly in a lateral direction. Appleby was about to call out that it would pass them by when a new, and very tiny, noise halted him. It was the yelping of a desperately frightened dog. And in another instant George appeared scampering towards the bungalow—the figure of George, his snowy fleece strangely metamorphosed to a dirty brown.

The dog ran up the veranda steps, sticky and dripping. Appleby stooped over him and whispered, "Oil." And in the same instant Diana saw his glance meet Dunchue's. It was an instant of blank revelation. She felt herself seized by the arm and propelled down the steps so violently that it was as if the cyclone itself had a grip of her. But it was only Appleby.

"Run!" he called; "run for your life!" Amid the uproar of the advancing storm there was yet another tiny noise—like the rattling of dry peas in a bladder. Something whistled by her ear. "Run," she heard. "Run!"

21

THEY WERE IN THE LONG TUNNEL OF GREENERY WHICH was the beginning of the road back to the hotel. It echoed with a dull growing reverberation, as if a train were approaching from a long way down a tube. Swift contrary blasts swayed the ferns and grasses, so that the tunnel appeared to rock like a device in a fun fair; they staggered dizzily down it, their senses further confused by a whip and scream of hurricane overhead. From all about them came the rending crash of falling timber; in front a lithe and bending palm snapped like a match; they scrambled over it and glimpsed before them what appeared to be the ragged stump of a pale-barked tree. The stump moved and Diana saw that it was one of Jenner's companions of the hotel; he was kneeling with some sort of dumpy weapon in his hands. Again she felt Appleby grab and they were crawling—crawling through a smell of earth and the clutch and scratch of undergrowth.

The crawl was desperate. It wrenched at her reason, so that she had to fight for her knowledge that these constricting bonds were blind nature and not the cast of cruel and cunning hands. They twined in her hair, trammelled a wrist, ripped at Miss Busst's pants. . . . And then the beach was before them; they were out on it and still only half in possession of themselves, half as twigs or leaves to the tyrannous strength of the storm. The wind roared more loudly; it blew and sucked like a vast defective bellows; the sea-apples danced between them like thistledown under a spell.

They joined hands and ran, ran as in some nightmare obstacle race in which there were thousands of punctured tennis balls under foot. Once more the peas were rattling in the bladder. Suddenly sand spurted up all round them— and Appleby halted her, stood still.

"Sorry," he said. "They've got us."

She looked over her shoulder. Certainly it was no good. They all had those dumpy weapons and they were less than fifty yards away.

"John—"

Uproar compared to which all before was silence drowned her words. Before her eyes Appleby's shirt turned into shreds and vanished. They were caught up, hurtled through the air, pitched down together yards away in a confused heap. She was on her hands and knees, aware of a sort of strange element about her. She gasped. All around them was one swirling and impenetrable curtain of sea-apples. Visibility was nil. The strange fibrous balls, large and small, wildly buffeted them. They were like dwarfs caught in a snow fight between giants.

Appleby took her hand again. "They can't see us. We'll go on." They staggered forward, as people might move in a great flying-boat out of control. The beach pitched itself at them in sudden bewildering angles; the air was filled with sand, with an acrid dust from the sea-apples; each breath was caught with pain. It was difficult to go on; it was impossible; they stopped.

The dance of the sea-apples, the drift and drive of the sand took on a pattern, a curve, a circular sweep. Everything was sweeping round them suddenly in a simple rhythm, round and round with increasing speed and an increasing density. They were sprawled, gasping, on a little island of stillness. And all around was a swirling cylinder of sand and sea-apples and twigs and leaves through which it would be impossible to plunge. They sat idle, like explorers in a little tent, held up by a blizzard. And somewhere—in a similar stillness, perhaps, or in the very chaos of the storm—the enemy waited too.

Diana panted. The air was thin and suddenly clear, as on top of a mountain. "John, what happened?"

Appleby grinned, exhausted. "We went to see Dunchue. We suspected he suspected we were suspecting, and we were going to persuade him that we suspected the wrong thing." His eyes, red-rimmed and strained, were striving to pierce the dizzying swirl before him.

"I know that. But—"

"But George gave the game away. Didn't I tell you he was vital? George and this fantastic storm. Between them they exposed the mystery of the dump."

"The what?"

"The dump. What our friends called the barrow or the tumulus or the dig. What Heaven thought was pirate gold. What we pretended *we* thought was pirate gold. What is really oil—thousands of gallons of it for submarines."

"John!"

"Just that. The cyclone ripped the sand from it and stove in a tin or so. Poor old George at his burrowing came in for an oil bath. And Dunchue and I looked at each other and it was all up. He just knew that I knew, and that we'd almost had him fooled. We ran."

"You knew all the time?"

"I thought it might be arms; I know there are plenty neatly cached about the world. Anyway, something they were just concerned to sit on. Theirs was a waiting game; I got that as we sat over our coffee yesterday in the bungalow. And the whole tempo of the island made it plausible."

"I don't understand about that chart."

"A third line of defence. If they were exposed as Pacific archaeologists they were after Vikings; if they were exposed as that they had ready a story—and a chart—of pirate treasure. I like Dunchue; I think he's thorough."

"At any minute he may be thorough again."

"Too right, Diana."

"The man's a murderer."

He shrugged his shoulders. "Theirs is an imperial theme. And we have to hold them up. Which, at the moment, means making the hotel." He got to his feet. "Above all this racket I can just hear the breakers still. Which is a guide of sorts. I think we'll try to get through."

They moved forward and were presently in the swirl again.

"I wonder what happens after this round-about effect?" Diana asked.

"Possibly very little. The island returns to normal. But I hope not." He glanced anxiously behind them; the sea-apples were beginning to fall and scamper about the beach again, so that the strange curtain which had cast itself about them was becoming thinner. "The elements be-trayed us. They have also saved us and for a time they must stay on the job. A fog or even sheeting rain would be capital. Or an earthquake or a tidal wave. Anything to provide cover and confusion to get us back and away. Now we'll run."

They ran, still almost blindly. To distinguish any sound of pursuit was impossible; a mechanized column might have been behind them and they would have been none the wiser. For the island was full of noises: of great water-wheels that creaked monotonously as they turned, of monsters crashing through the undergrowth or plunging into pools, of Cup Final crowds roaring goal, of twanging instruments mounting urgent scales. And all this was but a ground bass to the chant of the congregated demons of the upper air. This rose again in a clamour that might have cracked the welkin; King Lear in all his madness could not have bawled for a more clamorous storm. It was no longer possible even to shout; there was no longer any

question of hearing the breakers; but they moved down
the slope of the beach until they met the sea. It was then
comparatively easy to go forward in the right direction.
But this probably applied to the enemy too.

The storm, continuous overhead like a great slab of
chaos, was capricious and fragmented on the ground; suddenly they would tumble out of it into a drifting pocket
of sticky calm, and as swiftly it would be all about them
again; their progress was like a dream of struggling
through some horrid pot-pourri of clear and thick soups.
The uncanny effect intensified. To their left the air suddenly exploded and rocked them; the same thing happened on their right and they were drenched with spray;
straight before them sand leapt up like a roaring geyser.
A battlefield, Diana thought, must be rather like this—
and as the idea came to her she was swung round by
Appleby and they were making up the beach to where
the cover of the jungle lay. Dimly she realized what had
been happening. Something landed with a plop at her feet.
It looked like a cricket ball. They were past it, running.
She was pitched forward amid a whirl of force that hurt
the ears and lay covered in sand.

The world was still slipping slowly away behind her—
so they must be crawling still. Through undergrowth
again. And the jungle blanketed the storm; she could hear
Appleby shouting.

"They followed down the water's edge—chucking
grenades. But we're all right here."

"Had we better lie low for a bit?"

"No. We must try to make the hotel before them. Come on."

They went on. Diana felt soaked to the skin. Perhaps it was raining torrentially. Or perhaps she was bathed in sweat. Or in blood, perhaps, from an unfelt wound or from the prick and scratch of the thorns. But she could crawl. And then, unaccountably, they were on the little jungle path again and running. The soupy sand-charged atmosphere thickened and they were running blind. But almost they must be there. Diana felt a hard and artifact surface under her feet. Before she could think it had vanished and she was head-under in water. She clutched and grasped something flabby and yielding; for a second she thought of her companion by some powerful agency horribly pulped; she realized that she was in the swimming pool with her arms round a large rubber toy.

Appleby hauled her out. "You couldn't have done better. Gives us bearings. Come on." But the atmosphere was clearing again before some down-driving blast of wind and presently they could distinguish the outlines of the hotel. "Home," Appleby said.

The air was still clearer and the hotel thrust forward and defined itself before them like a shot in an arty film. They leant forward against the wind and stared at it distrustfully.

"A bit battered," Appleby said. "Position thoughtlessly exposed for weather of this sort. But we may make something of that." As he spoke a chunk of iron roof blew off and floated at them like a vast driven leaf or a flying carpet.

The hotel and its outbuildings stood on the neck of a peninsula with a little tongue of land, where the jetty lay, behind. It was impossible to approach it cautiously from a flank and they stepped boldly forward towards the front. There was no sign of life. Perhaps everybody was huddling in the most sheltered part. Or perhaps not.

They were on the steps. Something stirred—and Diana, recognizing it, jumped. It was George, his chrysanthemum fleece sadly bedraggled and browned. He rose, not without a remnant of dignity, to meet them. Diana patted him.

"John, do you think—?"

"No. They wouldn't have left him out here as a warning. We're first, all right. And George has come over to our camp. A countryman, after all. George, come along."

They skirted the verandas, all three, and ran towards the boat-house. Half way they met Miss Curricle, her clothes whipped about her by the gale, nubile again.

"Disgraceful!" she bawled at them, and gestured at the elements. It was plain that she had gone out of partnership with natural law and established herself trenchantly in opposition. "And virtually out of a blue sky. Cloudless . . . intensely blue." She plunged towards the hotel, the wind shoving and slapping at her from behind.

The boat-house was before them and they dived in. A figure like a nigger minstrel rose at their feet, crooked an oily finger within a collar that wasn't there.

"It reminds me of our organ," it said. "Sometimes we have discovered trouble within fifteen minutes of service. And knowing that the Tavenders were coming. Lord Tavender's father gave it to the church. Bought it up somewhere. Awkward." Mr. Hoppo giggled cheerfully. "*Parvis componere magna.* And I am delighted to see you back from your hazardous mission. George looks as if he had been engineering too." He flourished a spanner and disappeared.

Mudge's voice came from the bowels of the launch. "The transmission, Mr. Appleby; there's a little bit of trouble there. Shall we be wanting the craft soon?"

"At once, I'm afraid."

"Half an hour, sir."

"Very well." Appleby spun round as the door was tugged open from outside. It was Mr. Rumsby, agitated and determined.

"Look here, the electricity's still off. But there's a kerosene stove and I think I can manage a spot of dinner if—"

Appleby had pushed past him and was running towards the hotel. Diana followed. The guests were huddled in a corner of the lounge, rather like startled minnows in a pool. Glover was frowning over a shot-gun, the only weapon about the place which a search had revealed. And Sir Mervyn Poulish sat on a piano and sipped whisky, a sardonic spectator of the scene. Appleby strode up to him.

"Sir Mervyn, did you ever try arson?"

Poulish frowned in an effort of memory. "No"—he spoke rather regretfully—"I can't say I ever did."

"You have your chance now. The whole place must be an inferno within five minutes."

Poulish nodded and slipped from his perch on the piano. "Petrol," he said.

22

Had the guests of the late Mr. Heaven, before deciding to set out for their island asylum, thought to purchase some manual of elementary psychology they might have saved much in the way of diamonds and Triangular Capes. For they would have learnt that physical danger is often less daunting in actuality, when nature has poured appropriate chemicals into the blood, than it is in the prospect and when operative only upon the imagination. They would have learnt—so unsearchable is the human heart—that when one is oneself actively engaged there may even come certain rare moments to be classed among the Good Times. The guests were learning all this now. Mr. Rumsby, a wet towel tied round his dangerously open mouth, had made a brilliant sortie amid the flames to plug a gap with kerosene. Miss Busst was putting more vigour into rolling petrol drums than she had ever put into chasing fat gentlemen about the beach. The whole hotel had become a little microcosm of ordered national effort.

The fire was spreading to the jungle. It darted through the undergrowth with the swift sinuous movement of a snake. It scampered like a great golden squirrel up the trunks of dark-foliaged trees and set them suddenly ablossom with flame. The enemy advancing against this might have awkward moments. But it was only the line of the hotel itself and its half circle of out-buildings that formed for the time an impregnable barrier. To outflank this flaming mass they would have to swim. And against a swimmer was Glover and his shot-gun.

Diana had rolled out the last drum of sugared petrol and paused to view the leaping flames.

"John," she asked, "has it occurred to you that the wind may change before that launch is ready?"

"Don't worry. Unlike Poulish, I'm not a tyro. I often do this."

"Burn places?"

He smiled absently. "Well, once before. But on a smaller scale—and on an altogether more important occasion. . . . What do you think our friends are doing now?"

"Gone back to fetch something nasty."

Appleby nodded cheerfully. "They insured themselves against some of us attempting a getaway when they made their cannibal raid. Doctored the petrol and monkeyed with the magneto. So they'll think they can give half an hour or so to bringing up the Big Berthas. They will reckon, though, on a spot of hidden petrol and won't wait longer. . . . Ah!"

High above the clamour of the now dying storm there rose the crash of an explosion. Diana hitched up Miss Busst's tattered shorts and opened childish eyes. "They're not really shelling us?"

"Dear me, no. Grenades again—quite big ones. But that one was deliberately short of us by quite a long way —nerve-stuff." He turned round to the door of the boat-house. "How long now, Mudge?"

"Fifteen minutes, sir. But the old place will burn for longer than that."

"No doubt." Appleby was scanning the lie of the land anxiously. On one side were the flaming buildings; on the other were only the boat-house, a low concrete jetty and the sea. The jetty offered cover, and now at this first explosion Glover was shepherding the guests into a couple of uncomfortable feet of water behind it. The grenade had exploded beyond the burning hotel, but it would not be at all difficult for the enemy to get near enough to lob others over it. And they would only have a small area to destroy.

Diana was counting heads. "The native boys have bolted. Are you going to take everybody else away?"

"Everybody who prefers that to being taken prisoner." Appleby turned quickly at a warning shout from Hoppo. Quivering in the earth not far behind him was one of the familiar native spears. He ran to it and pulled it from the sand; there was a scrap of paper tied to the shaft. He tore it off and came back unfolding it.

"Unconditional surrender within five minutes and we shall be accommodated as prisoners in a supply ship when it comes in." He turned it over, fished out a pencil. "Dunchue has his canons. What shall we say?"

"Rule Britannia."

He scribbled, paused. "Mudge," he shouted, "pole her out to the end of the jetty; they know just where the boat-house is. Diana, join the others." He tied his message to the spear and waited with it poised.

Diana ran. The storm had cleared. Everybody was standing in tepid water, crouched against the solid concrete of the jetty. Mudge and Hoppo were shoving the launch towards them. And then Appleby came running and dropped down in the middle of them.

"Listen," he said. "This voyage is going to be at very great hazard. But here—"

He was interrupted by a flash of fire and the crash of an explosion. Another and another followed. They were deluged in sand and spray.

"But here behind the jetty anyone will be fairly safe. They'll stop this as soon as they see us at sea. Then it will be just a matter of being a prisoner. Intending travellers into the boat, please!"

Another salvo of grenades rocked them. Everybody was scrambling in. Twenty yards away the boat-house rose solidly into air, disintegrated, came down in a shower of dangerous rubble. Suddenly, as if an overmastering excitement had seized it, the launch throbbed and quivered. Mudge looked up triumphantly. "All correct, sir."

A grenade exploded in air. There was blood on the deck. The jetty veered away. Behind the launch curved a little line of foam.

"The reef," said Appleby.

It lay half a mile out. The channel through which they must pass was perhaps twenty yards wide. And leaping over the part-submerged rocks towards it was the figure of a man.

"Dunchue." Appleby turned to Glover. "Our efficient friend. He decided on that stance just in case. You must judge how long to hold your fire, sir."

Glover nodded. "I'm a fair shot . . . think I can beat a damned grenade . . . even on water. Mudge, whatever he does don't swerve till I've fired."

"Aye, aye, sir."

"Could do with a bullet—or a double-barrel. Best keep full speed ahead, Mudge."

"Full speed ahead, sir."

Glover lay down on deck. Dunchue had reached the tip of the reef and stood poised, waiting. It occurred to Appleby that he might have found a foothold deep in the water and lobbed his grenade from safety. But that would spoil his aim, and Dunchue didn't intend that. Now he was waving to them—waving them back. Perhaps he felt that Unumunu and the two men called Heaven were one thing and a boat load of silly women another. But he would act, all the same.

Within the reef the sea was almost calm; the storm was now no more than a continued strange appearance in the sky. The light was fair, and it favoured neither side. . . . The launch drove on, the open ocean before it and behind the Hermitage burning fiercely against a backcloth of jungle.

They were just short of the channel. Dunchue's arm came up and Glover fired. Dunchue staggered, crumpled, slopped in water. He rose to his knees, steadied himself, his arm flashed. It was all in split seconds. And in a split second Diana had dived low across the deck, scooped something, flung. Appleby had an instant's vision of white flannels, green turf, a crowd. The grenade exploded at Dunchue's feet. There was a leap of water and then empty sea.

The reef was behind them. They were on the Pacific again.

23

"But only," said Appleby, "he wasn't quite efficient enough. Or rather, he had at times a power of imaginative improvisation which got in the way of his efficiency. It wasn't really efficient to sham drunk before a trained observer; it was just a beguiling idea that came to him and which he had to keep up." Appleby was talking quietly, dispassionately, his eye on Diana. "And so too in the matter of Unumunu. When I showed I doubted the savages, he thought up something in an instant. Poulish had been in jail and was therefore a suspicious character. So he told us Yes, that the name Unumunu vaguely meant something to him but he couldn't remember what. And then a little later he spun you the yarn about remembering something about Unumunu and Kimberley on the radio, and about Poulish's being upset. As Poulish was known to have done some deal in diamonds and Unumunu at least originally came from Africa, it all had the superficial air of hanging together. But it wasn't really efficient. It was a quite unnecessary false trail, and it would turn suspicion back upon himself if by any chance Poulish and I could strike up a relation of confidence. It was unnecessary, as the story of Jenner kicking George was unnecessary. Eh, George?"

George, slightly sea-sick, closed a solemnly affirmative eye. But Diana did not smile. She was pale.

"I could just have thrown it into the sea," she said. "There was no need to chuck it back at him. It was a sort of re—" She puckered her brows.

"Reflex."

"Yes. It was just because at cricket you send the ball straight back to wicket. . . . I killed him."

"You killed him. But he had another grenade and might have got us with it."

"Yes."

"And for that matter Glover may really have got in before you. I doubt if Dunchue would ever have got back along the reef."

"Yes." She put up her chin and looked at the horizon. "Well, here we are again. Whom do you think I shall have to take a bottle to this time? Rumsby?" She smiled faintly.

Miss Curricle looked up from cautious overtures to George.

"Only in a sense," she said. "Here we are *almost* again. But at least this launch may decently be described as a *craft*. I never felt that an inverted café was adapted to navigation. And I inherit from my dear father a distaste for improvisations. You may not have felt the same. I have been told that Australians have a fondness for what they call *making do*. But for my part I say: simplicity, yes—but the ramshackle, no."

-C 233 >-

"We're not ramshackle," said Diana indignantly. "But if you had to live on the back-blocks—"

"Live on the *what?*" asked Mr. Hoppo courteously.

Appleby sighed. The horizon was very empty. Only directly behind them the island showed like a smudge on the ocean. Good-bye to Ararat. They were running due west and he turned to stare out over the prow. There was only the path of the declining sun. Of that land which had once miraged up over the horizon there was no sign. But then it had been vaguely spoken of as a hundred miles away. There could be no landfall yet.

The sea was sullen and working under a sky still faintly copper to the zenith; a haze was coming up from the north. Most of the guests had retired not too happily to the little cabin; fortunately their escape had been attended by no casualties worse than a gash or a scrape. And there was plenty of water and plenty of biscuit. Mudge had seen to that. Immediate anxiety must be concentrated on petrol and the weather. On that and perhaps the possibility of something unwelcome appearing on the horizon. For concealed somewhere in the bungalow or about the island those people must have powerful wireless communication. Or would they? Could one have wireless without giving such a secret depot away? Appleby moved aft to where Mudge stood at the wheel.

"Say something over a hundred miles," he said. "And then perhaps fifty miles circling round until we actually spot land. Have we anything like that range?"

Mudge shook his head. "Nothing like it, Mr. Appleby; it would be a picnic if we had. She's going at the economic speed now. But the swell takes it out of her. Eighty miles out of port all told. After that we might rig something to do about a couple of knots." Mudge's meditative eye went over his right shoulder. "And there's something coming up."

"Storm again?"

"No, sir. A kind of fog not uncommon in these parts. May hang about for days and give us no chance to raise a bit of an island at all."

"Awkward."

"We're well found, Mr. Appleby." Mudge was eminently placid. "Did you ever read Warton's *The Pleasures of Melancholy?* Screech-owls, sir, and mouldering caverns dark and damp. The gloomy void and hollow charnel. The still globe's awful solitude. Wan heaps. Atmosphere, Mr. Appleby. The solemn noon of night. There's expression, sir. The solemn noon of night. Elevated, Mr. Appleby; elevated, indeed."

Appleby thought it might more justly be termed depressed. But there was something soothing in Mudge's sombre-liveried culture-talk. And Mudge was going on to speak—more appropriately but hardly more cheerfully —of Falconer's *The Shipwreck* when there was a shout from Hoppo in the bows.

"Whale!" Hoppo was shouting with vigour. "Whale!"

Miss Curricle, now on established conversational terms

with George, looked up with justifiable alarm. Several people came out of the cabin. Appleby turned and followed Hoppo's pointing finger. And this time it was certainly a whale. The creature was blowing not a mile away; and presently a second whale could be distinguished behind it. In the emptiness there was something companionable in their mammalian spoutings; the launch was heading for them as if pleased to pass the time of day. And now more whales could be seen; it must be a school of considerable size; it occurred to some of the guests to express alarm. But Mudge would not be deflected from the course he was steering due west and the launch ran on unconcerned. It looked as if there would be a close-up view of the monsters as they puffed and vaguely shouldered the sea. And then, quite suddenly, the impending fog came down and they were travelling blind.

Mudge slackened speed. The guests retired again to the cabin. It had been broad daylight and soon it would be dark; meanwhile the fog produced an effect of untropical twilight upon the sea. It thickened until even the sound of the engine seemed muffled; over the bows the sun sank behind it in a dully diffused orange glow; from the cabin came a mumble and murmur of talk. And Appleby felt suddenly depressed. Perhaps it was Mudge on the pleasures of melancholy beginning to seep in; perhaps it was a sense that there lay something repetitive and dismally familiar in this wandering in cockle-shells about the Pacific. He was aroused by Miss Curricle's voice issuing from the gloom before him.

"Mr. Appleby," it said conspiratorially, "pray come here."

He crossed the boat. Miss Curricle was pointing with a disapproving finger beneath a thwart.

"I have no wish to cause needless alarm. But I have just distinguished an object which it is, I fear, impossible to contemplate without disquiet. In short, Mr. Appleby, a bomb."

Appleby peered. It was one of the enemy's grenades without a doubt, and must have landed plumb in the launch during the bombardment. Appleby looked at it with all the disquiet which Miss Curricle could have required. With the movement of the boat the thing was rocking gently on its base. It had all the appearance of being about to topple over at the next big swell. Appleby steadied it gingerly with his foot and called Glover. That Glover was not of a pre-grenade era he was uncertain. Still, he must be appealed to in lethal matter of this sort.

And Glover eyed the unambiguous object with respect. "A dud," he said. "There's just one thing nastier than a live bomb, and that's a bomb in a state of suspended animation. Better get it overboard." He stooped to put his hands cautiously about it; then he stopped, peered, chuckled and picked it up.

"We're slandering it: little chap never had a chance." He held it out before Appleby and a misdoubting Miss Curricle. "Like a Mills bomb—only bigger. You pull out a split pin before you throw. And an arm of the pin has broken off."

"Safe?" asked Appleby.

"We can easily make it safe. You have only to find a bit of wire while I hold down the lever."

"Then I think we'll keep it." He smiled. "And rank the launch as an armed auxiliary. A pity we haven't got an ensign."

Night and the sea fell together. The guests, grateful for an ocean of dim, dark-yellow glass, slumbered in the cabin. All around the fog was absolute, unstirred by any breath of wind. The only sounds were a lap of water at the bow and a gurgle at the stern—this and the throb of the engine. Mudge looked at his instruments.

"Best lay to, Mr. Appleby," he said. "By rights we should put out riding lights. But I doubt if whales and grampuses and the like would attend to them."

"The whales! You don't think they're about still?"

"Bless you, sir, I can hear them now."

Glover, crouched by the binnacle, grunted incredulously. "Hear them, my man—what d'you mean? Lowing? Growling?"

The sound of the engine died away, the lapping at the bows sank to a whisper. They listened. The night was utterly still. Oil might have been poured upon the water; there was only a long low swell which gently lifted the launch without breaking the sleeping surface about it. They strained their ears and heard nothing; relaxed and realized that there was something which they had been hearing all the time. It was low and vast, as if ocean sighed, weary of its own ceaseless flux. It was like a multitude of moans blended—as if one were hearing the muted despair of some circle of souls among the damned. It was the lazy, deep, long-drawn breathing of the whales.

And it was all about them. The launch floated amid a vast slumbering archipelago of living creatures, invisible beneath the fog which was their chilly blanket. For those who go down to the sea in ships, Appleby reflected, the story of Jonah may be an impossibility plausible enough. Islanded in the fog among these vast respirations, one could almost imagine oneself in the belly of the monster now.

"They must be dashed near." Glover, with an old campaigner's caution, spoke in a low whisper. "What about turning about and making off? Awkward if one took a lunge at us. Or suppose they like rubbing noses and we got in between."

Appleby laughed softly. "If only there were a tree."

"Eh? How the devil could there be a tree?" Glover quite failed to catch the allusion.

"As in the *Swiss Family*, sir. Hoppo's suggestion."

"Tscha! That was savages. No disgrace to bolt from brute beasts. But they seem to be all round us; best to lie low, no doubt. Hope that dog's asleep."

"We'll be all right, sir." Mudge was placid as before. "Short of a harpoon they're very sluggish, is whales.

Ruminative might be the word. A great deal of reflection in them, I'd say at a guess. And if you want to see one, sir—why, there you are."

They swung round at his words. Hard by the launch's starboard side, and where moments before there had been only a curtain of fog and night, there loomed and glided a shape vast, black and glistening. Absurdly, it seemed to tower in air like very Leviathan, as impossible as a creature of the Just-So stories. And then in an instant it was veiled and had vanished—vanished with a vast low *plop* like a pebble dropped in a well.

By the dim light of the binnacle Colonel Glover could be seen mopping his brow. Appleby still stared fascinated into the vacancy where the whale had been. It was like sailing the ocean of some mediaeval cartographer in which the monsters of the deep disported themselves familiarly around pygmean barques and galleons. To port he heard a hiss and ripple of broken water; another of the creatures must have returned to the surface from a nocturnal plunge. But this one remained invisible, and presently there was only the deep, low breathing of the slumbering school.

An hour passed—an uncanny hour during which it was difficult to believe in dawn. But dawn would come, and there was some petrol left, and conceivably they might make land. There were plenty of islands, Mudge said, though thinly scattered; they would come upon one with luck—an inhabited one if they had more luck still. He heard a slither in the darkness; it was Diana stumbling across the little deck from some hatch where she had curled herself.

"Mr. Mudge—John; whatever noise is that?"

"Whales, Diana. And setting you an example in the way of a good night's sleep. They don't even snore."

"Whales! I don't believe it." She stopped and stared into darkness. "Look!"

"I told you so." He turned round. Even closer than before, a vast shape had loomed up to starboard. It was a dull grey and rolling slightly. The water could be heard running down its great flanks.

Childishly Diana clapped her hands. "That island," she said; "it didn't have Hoppo's hippo after all. So this just *must* be Hoppo's whale."

Appleby laughed. "Very well," he said. "It's Hoppo's whale. Mudge says—"

He stopped. For out of the darkness Hoppo's whale was speaking.

"*Achtung!*" it said.

24

THAT HOPPO'S WHALE SHOULD INCONTINENTLY TAKE TO itself the character of Balaam's ass was a thing sufficiently astounding to ensure some seconds' silence. And by that time the truth was apparent and silence most evidently golden. Appleby leant down and flicked off the tiny light over the instruments. "Mudge," he whispered, "that coil of rope by the painter; how long is it?"

"Twenty fathom."

Appleby disappeared like a spectre towards the bows. The submarine appeared to be not under way, but the swell had carried the launch the few yards that made it invisible. There was the faintest splash forward and then silence except for the low heavy breathing of the veritable whales. Diana thought of how George might wake up and bark, of how Mr. Rumsby might wake up and vacantly curse the night. But everything remained utterly still; there was no further voice from the sinister craft beside them; Mudge and Glover were unmoving shadows by her side. Minutes went past. The launch rocked gently; Mudge was leaning out, hauling; Appleby, dripping and gasping, was on the deck. They waited and time seemed to linger about them as if trammelled in the fog.

Diana heard Mudge's whisper. "Clear of the screws and elevators, Mr. Appleby?"

"Jumping wire."

Silence again. She waited, expecting some terrific explosion. But when sound came it was the faint deep throb of Diesel engines. A voice called an order; the fog so muted it that it might have been the harsh cry of a bird. The noise of the engines rose, grew fainter. It could barely be heard. Silence. And then with a jerk the launch moved through the water.

Diana gasped. They were in tow. "John," she whispered cautiously, "I thought you would be doing something with that grenade."

She could just see him stir beside her. "No use. It might conceivably damage the steering-gear; nothing more. We want an open hatch."

"Will the rope hold?" asked Glover. "Forty yards seems rather a lot. Not that we couldn't do with a wider berth. Awkward if the fog clears."

"It should hold, sir. She's not likely to cruise beyond ten knots." Mudge was professionally knowledgeable. "We've just got to keep quiet and sit tight. Shh!"

The figure of Mr. Hoppo had emerged from the darkness, calling out with the somewhat uncertain cheerfulness which romantic adventure had induced in him. He stopped short at Mudge's hiss. "Whatever—?"

"Submarine," Diana whispered. "John 'has tied our painter to a submarine. And we're going for a ride."

"An *enemy* submarine?"

Appleby sat down by the darkened binnacle. "Well, they don't speak English. And we shall soon know."

"Dear me. If I remember my Greek a painter is really something with which one snares wild animals; it seems appropriate enough." Hoppo giggled, discreetly low. "Had not we better go round and enjoin silence? My memories of this launch are such that I feel they may set a gramophone going at any time."

"That dog," said Glover. "Perhaps best put him overboard, poor little beggar. Might give the show away properly."

"No, sir." Mudge was respectful but firm. "From a sailor's point of view I couldn't advise it. No good ever came of killing a living thing about a boat, begging your pardon. You may recall a poem about an albatross, sir. Picturesque, for the most part. But with a reflective strain to that effect, sir."

"Very well." Glover's agreement was perfunctory; he appeared to be thinking of something else. "I'll go round and warn the men, if Mrs. Kittery will do the same by the women."

Hours went past. The launch, silent, glided through the calm invisible waters as if propelled by a spirit of power. Faintly the sound of the Diesel engines could be heard from time to time. Presently, perhaps, they would halt and the submarine would go forward in short, cautious pushes. And that would be the ticklish period.

Appleby and Mudge had ready a pair of sculls; Diana had her hand on the tow-rope; immediately this slackened for more than a second they must silently and strongly pull. Otherwise with their light draft they might conceivably come up with the submarine as it stopped.

Dawn would have to be reckoned with soon, and the fog alone would be the riskiest cover to their manoeuvre then. But the darkness was still entire; the hours were lengthening themselves; the faint ripple at the bows sank as speed was reduced, and reduced again, on the craft before them. Presumably the cautious approach to fog-bound land—eerie in any circumstances—had begun. The launch moved; Diana would softly call; as softly they would pull at the oars. The submarine was nosing forward, stopping, nosing forward again. Once they heard a voice, startling in its brisk confidence, come clear down some crevice or funnel in the fog. Which meant, perhaps, that the fog would be breaking soon.

Glover was whispering in Appleby's ear. "Something on my mind. Are you proposing an operation for the destruction of this enemy force?"

Appleby turned in the darkness, surprised. "Yes."

"I don't know that I like it. Dashed good job, of course. But—"

"Our people must take the risk. They were warned of extreme hazards in the voyage."

"I'm not thinking of that." Glover appeared to have difficulty in expressing himself. "Mind you, it was all right with that fellow Dunchue. An officer, no doubt, and a brave man. But hanging about that island pretending to be tight, he was just a spy. Quite right to have done with him. But these fellows are regular sailors in a man-of-war. I doubt if they should be attacked except by armed forces of the crown. Worrying, Appleby—dashed worrying."

"Well, sir, you *are* the armed forces of the crown, are you not?"

"Retired list, my dear man. And then there's the question of uniform. Attacking force oughtn't to be in civilian clothes."

"I see." Appleby meditated suggesting that wars were no longer conducted on quite these lines. But he thought better of it. And Mudge broke in.

"Mr. Appleby, sir, I'm much in the same position as the Colonel. Naval reserve, sir. I'd be back now, if I'd seen my way to it. And I can do something in the way of uniform, having always kept my old kit in my own locker forrard. Nowhere safe from those copper-coloured vermin at the hotel."

"Give me your oar, my man, and cut along." Glover appeared greatly relieved. "Hullo, what was that?"

The submarine had given tongue—a melancholy sound like the last cry of a creature that has been long in pain. And from somewhere beyond came the call of an answering siren—a low blare, blurred and muffled.

"Of course," said Appleby, "it may be a depot ship. But I think it will be the island. And I'm not sure whether our first or second approach to it is the crazier. I can see a light. It must be something pretty powerful to pierce this fog."

"The fog's lifting." Diana's voice spoke from behind him. "Don't you think perhaps they'll wait till it's gone before going in?"

"They're going in now. Can't you smell anything?"

"Fog. And—and smoke."

"Just that. In fact, we're not a mile from Heaven's Hermitage Hotel. We're just off shore and running between it and the dump. You remember it's deep water at the dump, and with no reef beyond it. The light's clearer. They're flashing it from up on top, just about where we picnicked. Is that Mudge?"

"Aye, aye, sir."

"She'll be berthing in a minute. We must haul in until we're as close as we dare go. You'll take over; it's the sort of cast you're practised at. From the stern, I think, because the Colonel and I will scull her round for the getaway as soon as we're in position. Diana, as soon as the tow-line slackens next you tell us and then make for the cabin. No one's to come out. For whatever happens there will be a bang quite uncomfortably close. Everybody quite clear?"

They waited, listening to each other's breathing—and to their strained sense it was not unlike the vast respiring of the whales. To starboard was the deeper darkness of some near-by solid thing; before them was only fog and the shreds of night and occasional indecipherable sound. Suddenly Diana whispered, padded across the deck, and they felt the way of the launch slowly cease. It was motionless and they could see nothing—but when the fog cleared there would be the half-light of dawn. Appleby had the rope and was pulling gently in; there was more sound now—a clank and rattle and the calling of commands. Then the fog parted.

The fog parted like a contrivance of the theatre and close before them was the tail of the submarine. It lay berthed with its starboard flank rubbing the port fenders of a second submarine. And to starboard of that must be the dump. Arc lights of cold blue were slung from the conning-towers and from hatches aft rose a warmer glow. Men were moving on the decks, silently. And then from the shore—startlingly—there came a sudden laughter, deep and short. The sound served like some closing couplet on a stage. The scene shut as it had opened, and there was only fog.

They had been holding their breath—for it had seemed impossible that they had not been seen as clearly as they saw. But there was no sound of alarm; only from the shore a faint waft of singing, and now a muffled business-like voice from one of the decks in front.

But another break in the fog would be fatal. For already there had been a grey light, not that of electricity, over the momentary scene. Appleby murmured to Glover and they began with an infinite caution to turn the launch.

The movement lost them distance and they had to pull her awkwardly, stern first, towards the submarine. They could see the hull now, and the glare of the arc lamps beyond—and now they could see the light that beat up from the hatch.

Mudge was standing in the stern, something unfamiliar in his silhouette. They crept nearer. A voice spoke sharply, soberly: *"Gestorben?"*

There was a murmured reply, with here and there a word distinguishable: *". . . eine Granate . . . gestern abend. . . ."* Somebody hearing about Dunchue.

Mudge had his right arm flexed by his side. They sculled the launch yet closer and shapes loomed on the deck of the nearer submarine. The fog was shifting. Mudge waited. And suddenly the singing came clearly from the shore, rich, beautiful in the darkness.

> *"O Tannenbaum, O Tannenbaum,*
> *Wie grün du bist—"*

Diana felt Appleby tremble beside her. And then the fog had gone again and the submarine was very close and on the conning-tower was an officer turned away from them. And Mudge was shouting.

"Submarine ahoy!"

From somewhere a light flashed on him. He was standing in British naval uniform—a crumpled uniform made for a younger man; the light caught at his feet, swept upward to his collar with its braid of the Nile and Trafalgar.

Another beam sprang out, ran along the submarine's deck, flooded its after part with light. Men were shouting. Mudge's arm went circling in air. And Glover and Appleby drove with their sculls.

The explosion took the launch and bounced it on the sea like a ball; they were all tumbled against the thwarts and rolled in green water. But Mudge was at his engine and it had leapt to life. Waterlogged, they were running out to ocean.

Diana looked back and saw through the clearing fog a thin tongue of flame. It was half a mile away now, she thought . . . and then the same thing happened again. The launch leapt and shuddered; the roar of a vast detonation blasted them; the tongue of flame had become a waving curtain of fire. She turned to Appleby and shouted. She could not hear herself and shouted again. "What was that?"

"The first was just the grenade; that was the submarine." He was looking sombrely back across the sea. "Wait."

They waited. It was a matter of seconds before the second submarine went up too. . . . The grey light of dawn was about them. But they were unconscious of each other, staring back at the island.

Glover stirred. "Better do a bit of baling," he said quietly.

25

THE DUMP WENT TEN MINUTES LATER; EXPLOSION HAD wrought explosion with devastating effect. The dawn which they had supposed about them turned to darkness again. They were floating in a vast crepuscular region far into which struck light from one solid cliff of flame.

"Several birds with one grenade," Appleby said. "Including our own S.O.S. Until daylight it will be visible quite an astonishing distance. We must just hope it will stimulate curiosity. Our own cruising range is pretty limited now. Just about enough to take us back to the island. And, if nothing turns up, back to the island we must go."

"Back to the island?" Miss Busst turned from studying herself anxiously in a brass hand rail red from the distant fire. "Do you think they will all be—be dead?"

"Almost certainly not. We shall have to creep in by night and see what we can do in the way of stealing arms. Another whole cycle of adventure opening before us. Do you mind?"

Miss Busst considered. "I want to go home," she said.

"Ah." Mr. Hoppo, charitably engaged in expressing oil from George, looked up roguishly. "But our friends may be doing their best to keep the home fires burning too, you know." He giggled cheerfully at this grim pleasantry. "But I don't say you're not right."

They sat silent. Ineffectively at first and then with increasing success the dawn organized its own counter-demonstration to the vast conflagration behind them. And, as if loath to be overgone, the fire grew and mounted; perhaps, wind-borne over the sand-hills, it had got a grip of the jungle too. Miles out to sea though they were, it seemed incredible that they could not hear the roar and crackle of its progress, feel on their faces its dry, hot breath. Miss Curricle, who could be dimly seen to have returned by some magic to her everyday angularity, looked appraisingly back. After all, in this tremendous release of natural forces she really had some part; she could reasonably feel like an angel with a fiery sword.

"The flames," she said, "are gold and acid green and vermilion."

"Vermilion?" said Hoppo. "I do not know that I can distinguish quite that shade. I am chiefly struck by the appearance of intense white heat at the centre. And the periphery is flecked with violet and blue."

"Gold," said Miss Curricle, "and acid green. But if anything predominates it is vermilion."

Diana looked out with large vague eyes over the stern. "It's awfully impressive. Like—like a great bush fire at home." She sighed, suddenly as nostalgic as Miss Busst. "I never knew how nice the Yarra was, or the muddy old

Murray, until I had all this boring and uncomfortable sea."

The launch rose and fell softly on the waters. The sun was up. In the cabin there was a fuss of combing and powdering as broad daylight seeped disconcertingly in. The fire was still tremendous and now there could be seen above it a great pillar of black smoke, vertical, massive, and tapering to a shallow capital, like the last standing column of some gigantic Doric temple ravaged by fire.

There was a smell of singeing; Mr. Rumsby was emerging from the cabin, still bearing the evidences of his prowess in arson. He walked to the stern and stared long at the pall which hung over the stricken depot, the ruined cunning machines, the bodies of dead men. He turned round, his face clouded with doubt.

"I say," he said, "I've found a tin of sardines; do you think we might have them for breakfast? Or do you think" —his eye went gloomily back across the sea—"we had better not?" Nobody answered. He shook his head— sadly, in some obscure acknowledgment of his own enormous unintelligence—and drifted away.

The deck had begun to grow warm; Sir Mervyn Poulish dropped boldly overboard and bathed; Mudge rigged an awning. The sun climbed high.

It was noon. The island was below the horizon and there was no longer any sign of flame. Only the great shaft of smoke was taller, and at the top beginning to spread out like some swiftly burgeoning tree. There had been two meals of biscuit and water; somebody had started the gramophone and Miss Curricle had insisted that it be stopped again; everyone had become aware that the launch was overcrowded. Discomfort was in sight—and beyond discomfort the problematical. Appleby looked at the great crumbling tower of smoke. It was a magnificent signal still. But hours had passed—

There was a shout from Diana; people were pointing, running to the rail. A mote, a feather, a tiny cloud of smoke was on the horizon; it grew; there was a discernible form beneath it; it was a ship. A low, grey ship—and it raced towards the island, inquisitive, headlong, cutting its way between two gleaming walls of foam. It looked as if it would pass within yards of them; it was less than a couple of miles away and they would be under the gaze of binoculars now. There was a great deal of cheering and George stood up and wagged his tail.

"A destroyer," Glover said; "can anyone make out the flag?"

"The flag is a White Ensign."

"A White Ensign? I am inclined to think that it is an Old Glory."

"The flag is a White Ensign."

Diana patted George. "Anyway," she said, "it's a destroyer. So that's alright."

And Appleby sighed.

THE END

-⟨ 254 ⟩-